Dear James,
how far
the stories along the way. All
the best - love & happiness to you
and Maya
Marya

◇·◇·◇

# Peace Like a Monkey

*and other tales from life in Tanzania*

◇·◇·◇

**Marya K. Plotkin**

LYSTRA BOOKS
& Literary Services

Peace Like a Monkey: And Other Tales of Life in Tanzania
Essays by Marya K. Plotkin
© 2017 Marya K. Plotkin

ISBN print book: 978-0-9974484-7-4
ISBN ebook: 978-0-9974484-8-1

Library of Congress Control Number: 2017941612

Print books may be ordered online or through book stores. Ebooks are available for all devices and software.

A version of the chapter "Peace Like a Monkey" appeared in 2010 under the title "Monkey Business" in *Mama Dar: Tales of Family Life in Tanzania*, edited by Amy Gautam and Debbie Ventimiglia. Used by permission of the editors.

Back cover author's photo by Adrian Moreno.

All photographs are property of the author.

Book design by Kelly Prelipp Lojk.

**LYSTRA BOOKS**
&c Literary Services
WWW.LYSTRABOOKS.COM

Published by Lystra Books & Literary Services, LLC
391 Lystra Estates Drive, Chapel Hill, NC 27517
919-698-0415

*This book is dedicated to Dr. Gilly Arthur (1967–2014). Gilly was an exceptionally intelligent, intrepid, loving, and fun friend, mother, daughter, sister, and wife. While we miss her terribly, we remember her adventurous spirit with joy.*

# ⠿⠿ CONTENTS ⠿⠿

*Safari ni hatua*
*(A journey is made up of steps)*
– Swahili proverb

I learned the Swahili expression *safari ni hatua* from a taxi driver in Zanzibar. Its literal translation is: *A journey is made up of steps.* In colloquial use, it means *take it easy, one thing at a time,* or *first things first.* It implies a long journey and the need for patience. Don't worry, you will get there, every step brings you closer. I went to Tanzania first in 1992, when I was twenty years old. Between then and 2014, I lived for more years in Tanzania than I had in my native United States. When I visited my family in the States, I was a guest. When I returned to Tanzania, I was home.

But eventually, I came back to America to raise my two sons.

Of all the extraordinary lessons about life Tanzania taught me, the final one was perhaps most important. It taught me how to leave a beloved home. I am still learning.

# :::::: TANZANIA ::::::

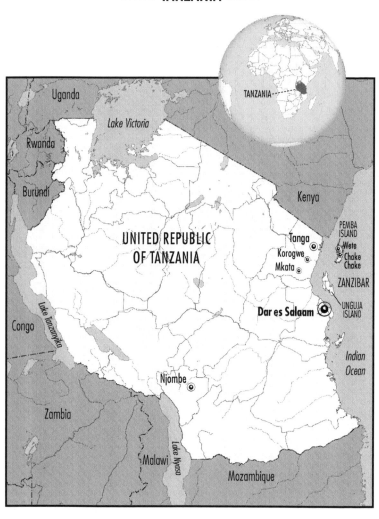

# ‡‡‡‡‡ USEFUL WORDS ‡‡‡‡‡

## Swahili and Tanzanian regional words

*Africafe:* powdered instant coffee, available everywhere in Tanzania.

*Bajaj, bajaji:* a smaller version of a golf cart, called a *tuk tuk* in many Asian countries. *Bajaj* is the brand name of the model sold in Tanzania. Swahili speakers do not like words that end in a consonant, so they add the final "i" to form the word *bajaji*.

*Bibi:* grandmother in Swahili. In Zanzibar, *Bibi* (abbreviated *Bi.*) followed by the name is a respectful way to refer to a woman.

*Boda-boda:* motorcycle-taxi, very common transportation option around cities. Notably rough driving.

*Bui bui:* a black whole-body cover worn over clothes by Muslim women.

*Chupi:* underwear.

*Dala-dala:* a mini-van or bus used for public transportation, manned by a driver (*dereva*) and conductor (*conducta*) who collects the fare.

*Dondosha Mkonosweta:* the first slogan for the male circumcision campaign in Iringa, translates into "roll up your shirt sleeve." Discontinued as a slogan in 2011, when a Ministry of Health employee complained that it was too informal.

**Kanzu:** the white tunic worn by Muslim men when going to mosque or on religious holidays.

**Karibu:** welcome. Likely the most commonly heard word in the Swahili language.

**Kanga:** a multi-purpose cloth wrap that comes in bright colors and designs and has a phrase or saying written on it in Swahili. Used to carry babies on backs or as a skirt and shawl and commonly given as a gift between women.

**Kifua kikuu:** tuberculosis (direct translation: big flu)

**Kofia:** a round hat worn by Muslim men.

**Konyagi:** local gin, produced in Tanzania, very inexpensive.

**Omo:** laundry detergent powder.

**Panga:** a machete. Staple of life in a village or rural setting. Used for cutting brush, firewood, killing snakes, or any similar necessity.

**Pole:** "so sorry, I empathize." The term pole has not a tinge of sarcasm, as "sorry" can have when used in English conversation.

**Watanzania, Mtanzania:** Tanzanian people, a Tanzanian person. The "wa" prefix in Swahili means multiple people, while the "m" prefix means one person.

**Wazungu, Mzungu:** Foreigners, a foreigner. Accounts of the origin of the word are multiple, but one theory is that the term comes from the Swahili word *kuzunguka* which means to travel or circle around. When white people came to the region for the first time, they apparently all looked the same to the Africans living in the region, who then thought that the same man had the ability to get around tremendous distances, *kuzunguka*. Another etymology suggests that the original white people who came to the region wandered around aimlessly. The term *mzungu* used to imply white people only, but more recently, all foreigners, including black people from other African countries, might be called *mzungu* as well. Indians and Chinese are often more specifically referred to as *Mhindi* or *Muhindi* and *Mchina*, respectively.

## Useful West Africa regional terms

*Dash:* bribe

*Fufu:* one of the staple foods of West Africa, this is a stiff porridge made out of either corn or cassava, which people eat with their hands with a soup, stew, or greens. In Liberia, *fufu* is made out of fermented cassava and is thus gluey and has a very sharp tangy flavor. It is not meant to be chewed, rather you break off a hunk, dip it in stew, and swallow whole. Liberians can be quite amused to see a foreigner chewing on *fufu*, making a face at the unpleasant taste.

*Pepper soup:* usually made with fish, a flavorful and extremely spicy broth with lots of the Scotch Bonnet peppers Liberians prefer.

# Leaving Tanzania

There is a difference between "going" and "leaving." I have come and gone from Tanzania many times, but I have only left once.

The first time I left a country in Africa, I was seventeen years old. I fled Liberia as a civil war intensified, on a plane going anyplace away from there. It happened to be Freetown in neighboring Sierra Leone. I walked off the plane, safe but with no idea what I would do. As a teenager, I thought I was getting on a plane to go somewhere, but in fact I was a bell resonating with the single tone of leaving—leaving behind the danger, leaving the fear, leaving the devastation.

It is only with looking back that I know that I wasn't going to Freetown, I was leaving Liberia.

In 2014, I knew without doubt, I was leaving my home in Tanzania.

I have learned, leaving means letting go. When I left Liberia, I was relieved to let go of danger and sorrow. When I left Tanzania, I was sad to let go of the comfort and joy of what had become home, and of years of friendships. I cried in my office as I threw cards, pictures, reports, and notes into a cardboard box, packing away years of work and relationships, friendships, and accomplishments. I had beers in plastic chairs on the beach with longtime friends, people who will never have the money to buy a ticket to the United States to come visit me, with all of us pretending that it was the ocean breeze that made our eyes tear up. I took the boys to visit Tanzania's most famous game parks, where Janusz adopted a praying mantis as a pet and Tadzio took lots of grainy pictures of wildlife on his cheap camera, and thought that the next time they saw a giraffe it would be in a zoo.

I took time to say meaningful goodbyes to friends, gave away my possessions. I felt I had measured the size of my sadness, had faced it, and had come to terms with leaving.

But I was wrong.

When I arrived in Chapel Hill, North Carolina, I was unprepared for many things: feeling like a deer in headlights at the grocery store from too many brands of cereal; not knowing the right thing to say in conversation; knowing the right thing to say but the words forming in another language; having a commentary in my head about the ridiculousness of how people were acting, including my friends; being two beats behind in conversation both because of rusty English and because conversations in Tanzania were so much slower; and perhaps most difficult, feeling unease with where I lived. I was not at home.

I missed warmth, in two senses. I never complained about the heat in Dar es Salaam: I loved it. For the first year in the U.S., I only felt warm enough standing in a hot shower. When I smelled the shampoo, its synthetic tropical scents reminded me of what used to naturally waft by in the evening air. My lips cracked in the cold, dry air. My ice-cold toes at night confirmed for me that mankind evolved in and for warmer climates. No one had cold feet in the Ethiopian cradle of mankind. In bed at night, I listened to the rainfall and thought, *what wimpy rain, someone turn up the pressure.* As soon as I got used to one season, it shifted and all of a sudden I did not have the right clothing for myself or for the boys. And in that first year, it only seemed to get colder, and colder, and colder.

More profoundly, I missed the human warmth. Tanzanian culture is sunny; the concept of a bad hair day or being grumpy simply doesn't exist. The norm of good humor was good for me, driving my inner cynic deep underground. I missed warm greetings in the morning; lingering, drawn out conversations that no one wants to leave; bosomy hugs from the colleague who had designated herself my Tanzanian mother; friends who delighted in tearing me away from my ridiculously American habit of eating at my computer and competed for the prize of buying me lunch.

Once the true impact of leaving Tanzania hit me, I was ironically in a state of discomfort in the midst of comfort. I was hounded by nostalgia and longing. It took almost a year for me to turn my back on nostalgia. Now I shake my fist at nostalgia. I challenge the evolutionary biologists to describe its competitive advantage. I think it was just some extra neurons left over after the really important things were established, like fight or flight and empathy. But like depression, nostalgia is real and oppressive.

Moving to the U.S. felt like sinking into a cushy easy chair; everything is so easy… and so boring. Let me explain how it is to pay the electric bill in Tanzania compared to the United States.

In the United States, my phone makes a discreet sound when my bill is due and a little notice pops on my screen. I enter a password, click on the "pay bill" icon, decide if I want to donate some extra money to charity; I have paid my bill.

In Tanzania, this would be a typical scenario: It was a Friday afternoon. I overheard a colleague talking about how much time he wasted collecting his bill from Tanesco, the power company. The previous month they had instituted a policy of having every client come to the office to pick up their own bill. Except they didn't tell clients about it. Instead, they published a notice in the paper. So now in addition to the massive queue to pay your bill, there is an equally massive queue to pick up your bill. Hours and hours of waiting.

Hmm, I thought. I haven't paid my bill in a while, have I? I called home, and sure enough, the power had been cut. And would remain cut all weekend unless I figured out a way to pay my bill in a few short hours. I made my apologies and left the office for the day, swinging into action.

Here was my plan: our neighbor's gardener, Owen, had a cousin who worked for Tanesco. I called the neighbor and asked if I could pay for Owen's time to go down to Tanesco to cut the massive queue of people desperate to pay their bill before the weekend. He agreed, and Owen said yes. The clock was ticking, and a weekend without electricity was just around the corner. We gave Owen some money for his daughter's school fees last month, so I knew that he would come through for us.

I texted my favorite *bajaji* driver to take Owen to the Tanesco office, but his vehicle was not on the road after being rear-ended by a car the previous week. I conveyed my condolences and asked about his wife, who was pregnant and sometimes cleaned my friend's house. We had a good laugh about a mutual and chronically tardy friend who he recently took to the airport. As we chatted on speaker phone, I texted Owen to take a *boda-boda* instead.

I had to go back to the office to charge my phone, because the battery was low and, well, I had no electricity at home. I got through to Owen and he had gotten the bill. It was for two months and it was a small fortune. Damn it, the billing address still read The Royal Dutch Embassy, since a diplomat from the Netherlands rented our house before us, and that meant they were still charging electricity at a diplomatic rate. (Yes, there is such a thing, and yes, it is higher.)

Owen got to his cousin and she agreed to discount the bill by 30 percent, which meant I had to get more money to Owen in thirty-eight minutes, because Tanesco didn't accept partial payment.

I drove to the closest ATM, even though I had heard that armed bandits had robbed it the week before. I squeaked the correct amount out of my account, just under the withdrawal limit for the day, parked my car at my friend's hair salon because I knew there was no parking at the Tanesco office, and hiked the money over to the office. I met Owen outside and transferred the cash from my pocket to his at 2:52. Tanesco closed at 3 p.m. Owen disappeared into the building and I kept my fingers crossed as I waited.

At 3:22 a guard let Owen out of the locked office. He nodded and smiled at me as he walked out, and I gratefully topped him up with some weekend beer money. When I got home, the lights were on. I had paid the electricity bill.

Two experiences with bill paying. Some people might conclude that the process is better in the U.S. But in Tanzania, the process allowed me to have pleasant conversations with multiple people, call in favors from a couple more, afforded a more marked beginning to my weekend, and allowed me to leave the office early on a Friday. More efficient in the U.S.? Definitely. Better? Depends on your perspective.

# Helping

In Tanzania, I could save a life every day. Not a day went by when I didn't do something for a person in need. Raise money for the gardener's wife who needed surgery. Help a friend who needed cement to build her house. Buy an extra loaf of bread to give to the underpaid guard at our gate. Helping people was addictive for me, and powerful. It was not fair and not right that I had so much privilege and so many resources, but didn't it feel like the best thing I had ever done to step in and play savior for someone in need? So much need, so many opportunities to help, so many chances to feel good about myself. Distorted, strange, satisfying beyond measure. In America, everyone takes care of themselves. I am not really in a position to help anyone. And no one is asking for my help anyway. Most Americans seem extremely distrustful of either asking for or being asked for help.

Here in the United States, I watch my friends toil with sanitized dilemmas, such as how to avert tedium, or how to get the best out of the free educational system for our kids. Here, I am infuriated when I have to call the insurance company three times to follow up on a claim. Meanwhile, my Tanzanian friend had her two front teeth knocked out in a crowded public bus when the guy in front of her slung his bag over his shoulder and hit her in the mouth. My nanny spent a year studying for her high school equivalency exam and was given the wrong exam from the Ministry of Education and failed, as did all the other adult learners in the country taking the exam that year. People's problems in the U.S. seem, well, first world.

Losing my ability to help people in a profound way took something out of me for that first year, but I came to understand, helping people is not just something I needed for my self-esteem; it is an essential part of being the person I want to be. My years in Tanzania taught me, friends helping friends, community helping community, is essential to everyone's survival.

I built myself back up by finding some volunteer work that felt meaningful, helping organize a day when kids got to spend time with their dads who had been incarcerated. Then I found my friend Mariela, who really did need my help, and who I could turn to for help. Her strong hands could change my car tire in minutes, and all I had to do was ask.

Home is where the heart is, but home is also where I am needed, and where I have people I can turn to for help. Home is where I have the power to make a difference in people's lives.

# Flying High

The pilot turned off the fasten-seat-belts light and let us arrange ourselves for the hours of our overnight flight. I was going back to Tanzania for the first time since I moved away. Today's departure was rushed. I went over long lists of things for the kids to do and not do with my parents, stocked the kitchen with food, filled the car with gas. By the time I got around to packing my bag, I couldn't find either the right clothes or the right feelings to pack for the trip.

The mixed emotions roaring in my head were as impenetrable as the constant hum of the airplane. Was that doubt? Excitement? Longing? I did not know how I felt, other than being in a state of anticipation. I adjusted the airplane pillow, leaned against the window, and tried to catch some twilight sleep. I hoped to wake up with all this confusion resolved.

Every Tanzania-bound traveler knows the feeling of walking off the plane in Dar es Salaam. The air hits your face with the impact of a warm and slightly damp blanket. For me, the first breath evokes half a lifetime's emotions and memories, in equal measure reminiscent and alive. I followed the herd of plane-ride-stunned people down the steps to the immigration office. I waited for the lady in a blue uniform to return my passport, I heard the banter of the men and women of the immigration office in Kiswahili, and I still didn't know how I felt.

The next morning, I awakened to a rooster crowing. I saw verdant green leaves shifting outside the window, stirred by a breeze, pierced by an unhesitating beam of sunlight. Africa was awake, as it always is at 7 a.m. I heard the sounds of a broom sweeping, a woman's voice singing, men joking over a gate. *This is no time for sleeping*, the rooster insisted, *it's morning.*

And then, I knew what I was feeling.

I was home.

Upon leaving Dar es Salaam a year earlier, I vilified the city. I magnified the crimes, as I had minimized them while I lived there. The drive-by car robberies always resulted in injury, and in the 3 a.m. burglaries, guards were hacked with machetes. In my mind the potholes deepened and the power outages made life impossible. The traffic was insane and made everyone crazy.

Some I did not need to magnify: a week before my return, a dear friend was shot by thugs robbing a store and was flown to South Africa for medical treatment. I found myself agreeing, albeit with a sense of guilt, when friends who had also left Dar said, "We got out at the right time."

But now that I was back, I saw all of those things existed, and yet the boats glittered on the ocean beyond the silhouette of palm trees. The fragrance of gardenia filled the air. Friends embraced me, the friend who I held for support at the side of another friend's grave, the friend who squeezed my hand tightly as her baby was delivered, the friend who attended my father-in-law's memorial service when I could not make it. Strangers greeted me warmly, laughter and enjoyment of life was everywhere, and the familiarity an antidote to my confusion. The language I worried would be gone bubbled up and rolled off my tongue.

I was home.

I needed to know that. I need to know that there is still somewhere in the world that feels like home. Even if that somewhere is half a world away from North Carolina, and even if I may never live there again. Home is not simply where I live, even if I have lived there for a whole year. Rather, *home* is a combination of familiarity and the illogical pulling of the heart, something like falling in love. People can be as illogical in their choice of home as they can be in the choice of a lover, picking the oddball over the safe bet, staying even after being knocked around a bit.

The realization that I do have a home in this world freed me from the idea that North Carolina must be home. I don't have to fall in love with North Carolina. We can be friends.

And hey, it's good to have friends, too.

# Setting my African Compass from West to East Africa

**From the *Chicago Tribune* (May 2, 1990)**

WASHINGTON – The United States has suspended the Peace Corps program in Liberia and told American diplomats they and their families may leave the country as fighting between the Liberian army and rebel forces increased, the State Department said Tuesday.

In addition, the department recommended that other U.S. citizens in Liberia consider leaving because of increased instability.

About 80 of the 135 Peace Corps volunteers assigned to the country have left, and Peace Corps officials said the others will leave by the end of this week.

Lee Raudonis, a spokesman for the Peace Corps, said it is unusual for the agency to withdraw its personnel. The last such evacuation was in December 1987, when the Peace Corps withdrew from Haiti, he said.

My road to Tanzania was a long one, and involved another country: Liberia. The path started in 1989 when I was sixteen and dissatisfied, an overly confident teenager who disliked high school. My Quaker parents had raised me outside of the mainstream. For many of my fellow teens, rebellion meant drinking and smoking pot; adventure meant a study abroad field trip in college. For me it meant leaving high school a year early and going to Africa.

In the public library, I came across a binder with a photocopied brochure for a volunteer youth program in West Africa called International Christian Youth Exchange, and a few months later I boarded a plane bound for Amsterdam and then Monrovia, Liberia. I celebrated my seventeenth birthday with new friends from my host family, on a beach outside Monrovia. I met a tall, blonde Danish girl with a quick smile and an uncommonly developed streak of good sense. Little did we know how much that good sense would be needed. Dorte Møller Hansen was nineteen and another volunteer. She became my best friend and traveling companion for almost a year. We were placed together in a town called Ganta, in northeast Liberia, just a few miles away from the border with Guinea. We lived at Ganta United Methodist Mission guest house and taught six-year-old children supplementary classes in writing and math at the mission school.

While Dorte and I loved our time in Liberia, the organization that had brought us there was less than organized and never paid us the stipends we were supposed to receive. We lived on a very, very small budget, which approximated, at times, the typical Liberian's. Lack of funds did not stop us from having fun, since walking around markets in town was free, as was going out to local discos where Lebanese merchants would buy us drinks, or catching rides on the back of Peace Corps volunteers' motorcycles. We went to local joints to eat steaming plates of rice with palm butter and cassava leaves, so spicy from the Liberian Scotch Bonnet peppers that tears ran down our faces. Our favorite local eating spot was one where the ceiling was decorated wall-to-wall with egg cartons. We got on buses to travel to other towns in Liberia, and met interesting people, Liberian and expatriate. By the side of a pool in Gbarnga, a mining town, we met a Danish biologist, Dan Meyrowitsch, and a Danish medical doctor, Kim Davis, who worked in a town called Zwedru.

At Christmas time, after a semester of working at the mission school, Dorte and I traveled by bus to Abidjan to visit a handsome young businessman who had passed through Ganta. Ahmed Koné was doing trade in car parts in Liberia and ended up in Ganta. He didn't speak English and was happy to meet two young ladies with high school French. Upon his departure, he invited us to visit his family in Abidjan, capital of neighboring Ivory Coast. When we arrived, we were wide-eyed in the beautiful city. After half a year in a Liberian town, Abidjan, with its ferries, cathedrals, and night markets, looked like Europe to us.

However, while we were in Ivory Coast, an event occurred that marked the beginning of the end of Liberia's stability for the next fifteen years. On Christmas Eve, 1989, Charles Taylor led a rebel invasion, starting in Ganta, the town in which Dorte and I lived. Presumably he launched his invasion in Ganta because it was close to the Guinea border and there was a tarmac road leading to the capital, Monrovia.

While Dorte and I had enjoyed the warmth and friendliness of life in Liberia, we knew that political tension was simmering. The atmosphere in Ganta had been, since we arrived, one of both dissatisfaction and fear of expressing criticism about the government. The famous execution of President Tolbert and his cabinet on the beach had taken place only nine years previously, and Tolbert's executioner, Samuel Doe, had been president since that time.

Dorte and I were about four hours outside of Abidjan, headed to Mali as tourists, when our bus broke down. We disembarked and camped outside waiting for a replacement to arrive, lying on a borrowed prayer mat in the grass by the side of the road. An older gentleman had a radio and we heard the familiar three tones which always preceded a BBC broadcast. Our blood turned to ice as we struggled to make out the details of the news in French, but we understood that the news wasn't good. We begged the man to find an English broadcast, which confirmed the news of a rebel invasion in Ganta, Liberia. We abandoned our trip to Bamako and hitchhiked back to Abidjan. Upon our return, we met John, Dorte's Peace Corps boyfriend, who had been with us in Abidjan and had taken a bus to Liberia at the same time we got on a bus towards Mali. He had reached the Liberian border to witness thousands of Liberians streaming out of the country on foot, their possessions in bundles on their heads. There was no more overland entrance into Liberia from Ivory Coast.

When I recall my seventeen-year-old self deciding what to do at that point, I am amazed at my inability to perceive danger. But it was such a different time, and the difference is not just me being a teen then compared to being an adult now. Without constant newsflashes, cell phones, security camera videos, and the internet, without threats of terrorists and airport security, the world seemed much safer. Dorte and I were faced with the decision: should we go back to our respective countries, or return to Liberia?

We remembered the warm smiles of our Liberian friends, the good food and fun adventures—we didn't think of violence, savagery, men with guns, and child soldiers, all of which happened in the upcoming years.

We pooled our money and bought air tickets back to Monrovia, ready to start again with whatever we had in our backpacks.

Thus started a second phase of our time in Liberia. We couldn't go back to Ganta. Dorte decided to go live with John, who was moved by the Peace Corps to what was thought to be a safer location in Gardour. I decided to try out life in a coastal town called Greenville, a sleepy fishing town with a small but international port, where I lived in the spare room of a Peace Corps volunteer named Lorrie.

Lorrie connected me with a friend of hers, a Philippino who ran the clinic of a logging company. He gave me a dubious job organizing the clinic's medicines, in hopes of bedding me.

After a couple of months in Greenville, I decided to look up Dan Meyrowitsch, the Danish biologist. He was working on schistosomiasis, also called bilharzia, a parasitic disease carried by freshwater snails. Dan and his colleague, Kim, had a lab set up in Zwedru, which happened to be the then-President Samuel Doe's hometown. Zwedru was three or four hours' drive from Greenville, an easy distance for me to catch a ride.

I spent some time with Dan catching snails in streams in villages around the town for dissection in the lab, and I developed an interest in science.

While Dan and I worked on his research projects, the rebels continued their steady advance on Monrovia. On my return visits to Greenville, it was very apparent that the situation was worsening. There was no more rice. Everyone was eating fish and pepper soup and cassava *fufu*, and beer was in short supply. Riots had occurred twice, with crowds of people hunting down members of President Doe's Krahn tribe. In one of these incidents, I had to take cover in the logging company compound as the frightening noise of violent hatred raged outside the locked gates. I could see these signs, but I didn't relate this with danger to myself.

While I was at Dan's I got the news that Lorrie had been

evacuated. Finally, it dawned on me that it was time for me to go. I caught a ride on a truck for the three-hour drive back to Greenville, arrived to find a deserted house, packed up a few belongings and begged a flight on the logging company's private plane going to Monrovia. There was only myself and a buck-toothed Israeli pilot, who seated me in the copilot seat and kept putting his hand in my lap as the two of us flew to Monrovia.

I learned later that there were 5,000 U.S. citizens in Monrovia then, all trying to leave. I am sure I was the only unaccompanied seventeen-year-old among them. A couple of days after arriving back in Monrovia, I stood in the rain and watched the receding flashing lights of military vehicles escorting my Peace Corps friends to the airport. I stayed with my host family and every day for two weeks, I visited the same bureaucratic office trying to get an exit visa. With no money to pay "dash" and not enough money to get a ticket to Europe, I didn't get far.

Now I was desperate to get out of the country. My host father intervened and bought me the exit visa and a ticket to neighboring Sierra Leone, from where a month later my parents were able to fly me back to the U.S.

Meanwhile, as I learned many months later, Dan had similarly decided that he needed to get out of Zwedru. He and Kim packed supplies and data into the project's Land Rover and made it to Greenville with only one attempt by drunk soldiers to confiscate the car. He and Kim found the situation in Greenville dire. They convinced the Danish captain of a fishing boat called Ocean Tramp that they needed a ride out of the country. They spent ten days at sea on the Tramp, which had electrical problems and not enough drinking water. Dan refreshed low food stocks on board by catching a large tuna using a coat hanger and a piece of red towel as bait. Kim suffered from severe sea sickness and lost over twenty-two pounds on the journey. When they arrived at the Canary Islands, they were received as refugees by the Danish consul.

All of this, I discovered after arriving back in the U.S. Dan and I were in touch for a while, but eventually the postcards I sent to his parents' address in Brønshøj, Copenhagen, went unanswered.

I arrived back in the United States as a seventeen-year-old who had been through a civil war. It pushed me further away from the path of being a mainstream American teenager.

By the end of the Liberian war, half of the population was displaced or killed. To heal my emotional shock and trauma, the pain of knowing those young children we had taught at Ganta United Methodist Mission were in devastating situations, I moved to an organic vegetable farm in Virginia. The simplicity of picking vegetables and sleeping in a barn lulled me and detached me from those difficult images and memories. My circuitous route took me next to New Jersey, where a serious boyfriend helped me gain some understanding of men and relationships, followed by months of working at a small, family-owned metal foundry in the Catskill Mountains.

In 1992, I started college. Marlboro College in Vermont was a group of white barns converted into classrooms atop a mountain dotted with apple trees, a college where smart and quirky young people came to learn.

And then came the letter from Dan the Dane. Africa calling, collect. A blue and white airmail letter found its way to my college box in Vermont from Tanzania, East Africa, with tales of the ocean, mountains, parasites, research, and a language called Swahili.

After a year in Denmark, Dan went to Tanzania to study lymphatic filariasis, a mosquito-borne parasitic disease that causes elephantiasis and hydrocele, a condition in which men's testicles swell. The condition was treated with diethylcarbamazine (DEC). As he described it, Dan drove around the mountains in the Tanga region taking blood draws at night and measuring men's balls. Could I come work with him? He would put me in a village where the villagers were using DEC-medicated salt. My job would be to stay in a village and measure salt intake in cooking to get an indication of dosage.

What nineteen-year-old could refuse? I didn't. Marlboro College agreed to give me credit for working on Dan's project for a few months, and by September I was on my way to Tanzania for the first time.

Even during my year of exploration and recovery in the U.S., my compass was skewed towards Africa.

In Liberia, I had been innocent. I had found adventure, but also conflict. In Tanzania, I found peace. I remember being in Dan's "salt village" in the verdant Usambara Mountains, punctuated with stately trees, thinking with a kind of reverence that if I came back to this spot a hundred years from now, it would still look the same. I know now that change comes to every corner of the world, even the slopes of the Usambara Mountains. But at the time, it fulfilled for me a deep urge to see Africa at peace. Maybe I could grow up here without trauma.

I have never been back to Liberia since the day in June 1990 when I boarded that plane to Freetown. It is not my African home. But I never would have had Tanzania as my home had it not been for that year in West Africa.

# Dar es Salaam

# 1

# A Career in Trading and Futures on the Streets of Dar es Salaam

From 2002 until 2005, I commuted for work from Masaki to Mikocheni, which, in those pre-traffic-jam days, was a fifteen-minute drive. It was on that commute, at the St. Peter's Church intersection, that I got to know two men I thought of as career roadside sellers. One of them, a man I named Forever-Young, sold magazines and the other, Squishy-Face-Funny, sold newspapers.

I was a sucker for Squishy-Face-Funny. He had a twinkle in his eye and a knack for making me laugh. As soon as he spotted my car rounding the curve leading to the intersection, he started exaggerated motions to let me know that he was going to sell me a paper if he had to run a marathon to catch up to me. If the light turned green and I couldn't stop, I would shake my head and my finger at him and frown largely, pantomiming, No, no, no, not today! But no matter which hand signals I employed, when I looked in my rearview mirror, I would see his gangly figure loping crazily through the intersection, and I would sigh and pull over. A minute later he appeared with a big grin on his face and I bought his paper. Then we had a healthy and happy few minutes, chatting about the weather or current events.

One Monday, I pulled up at St. Peter's and Squishy-Face-Funny was not there. I checked by the side of the road, where he sometimes went to restock from the papers he had stashed under a tree. Not there either.

Forever-Young stood on the median selling magazines in his lazy way. I rolled down my window. "Hey, where's the other guy, the one who sells newspapers? (*Yule jamaa mwingine, anayouza magazeti, yuko wapi?*)"

"*Amefariki*"

"*Amefariki?*" I repeated back dumbly, as if he could possibly have meant something other than what he said: He died.

"Yes, he got sick over the weekend and he died. Malaria, plus five." He added the test result for emphasis, referring to the density of parasites in the blood sample.

Just like that? A young man, healthy albeit skinny, gone just like that?

Wait, hold on, "*Ngoja, ngoja.*" I stalled to let my brain try to catch up with what I was hearing. "Did he have kids? *Alikuwa na watoto?*"

"Yeah," was the answer. "Three. Youngest just born last year."

Then the light changed, and I had no choice but to drive away, puzzling at the ragged-edged conundrum that had just been handed to me.

I knew Squishy-Face-Funny for years but I never asked his name. If you add up the two and a half minutes of cheerful discussion we had every morning, I probably interacted with him more than with some of my closest friends. He was so friendly and happy to see me that I forgot that he was poor, standing out in the sun and rain by the side of the road to sell newspapers for a few cents profit. In fact, he was so poor that he likely died because he couldn't afford the medical care he needed. What did I do for him? What was I thinking, how sustaining it is to have a laugh in the morning? How sustaining is it when you have plus-five malaria and no money to pay for the medicine? How could I have overlooked the fact that he was so poor?

Because of Squishy-Face-Funny, I began to greet career road-side sellers whom I recognized, ask about their health, buy what they were selling, and tip them when I bought something. Not all of them. But there are plenty in Dar es Salaam who I know by face since I have been driving by them for years.

In 2015, my commute changed and I drove a carpool of kids to school, traveling along Ocean Road. My career roadside sellers along this route were two men selling newspapers, Light-Skinned-Taller and Round-Faced-Dark. I would round the curve towards Selander Bridge and see my guys walking up and down the line of queued cars. In those traffic jams, they were there with a cheerful greeting, happy to see me whether I bought anything or not. They forgave me when I left my wallet at home, giving me the newspaper to pay another day.

I would roll down my window and we would chat about the weather, our families, and whatever else we had time for, while my school-bound kids in the back seat stared sleepily out the window. When a break in the traffic came, the restless crowd of cars surged forward, I rolled up my window and drove off with a feeling of having spent time with a friend.

One day in 2015, I rolled down my window to buy a paper from Light-Skinned-Taller. I liked him for his calm demeanor and shy smile. He was sweating and looked very tired. I asked how he was doing. He hesitated, looked at the long line of idling cars, looked back at me to gauge my interest. He then told me, he found out two weeks earlier he had *kifua kikuu*—tuberculosis. I asked him whether he was on treatment.

He explained that he traveled an hour to a clinic in Temeke once a week to get the medicine he took daily. I heard the rumble of cars ahead of me moving forward. I dug in my wallet and found a 10,000-shilling note, thinking, shit, what's the right amount to tip a newspaper guy who just told you he has TB? I found another 5,000, handed it to him and drove away.

I had a whole week before it was my turn to drive the carpool again. A whole week to think about this guy and what I could do for him, what I should do for him. There are many poor people with TB in Tanzania. I knew some of them in a much more established way than I knew him. Why should I help this guy? Because he sold me newspapers? Because once, years ago, one of my other newspaper guys died?

The next time I drove to school, I was prepared. I had my name and phone number written on a slip of paper. I asked his name so that I could think of him as a person rather than what he looked like. I put him in my mobile as *Rashid\* Newspaper* and sent him messages to ask how he was doing. I learned how to transfer money by mobile phone. While our initial chats were about the side effects of the medication and hardship his family was going through, eventually the calls became more spontaneous, and once I got an invitation to a church concert at which Rashid played the keyboard. When I saw him on the traffic queue, his smile for me was no longer shy, but very warm.

I began driving in Tanzania in 1992, and took to the streets as a commuter in 2000. Along the way, I changed from a young woman on an adventure to a person with an established career in public health, a wife, and a mother. As I grew up and my life changed, Rashid also started a family and established his career selling newspapers for pennies of profit.

For all of our differences, our lives crossed. We shared a history, and thankfully, by then, I had learned enough to recognize that point where shared experiences, openness, need, and generosity all came together.

---

*Not his real name.*

# 2

# Synchronized Turning

My years of driving in the United States prepared me somewhat, but not entirely, for driving in Tanzania. Learning to drive in Dar meant getting in touch with a thuggish and aggressive side I didn't know I had. Dar es Salaam is nicknamed *Bongo* (brain), which, some say, is short for "*Chemsha Bongo*" (boil your brain), referring to how you feel trying to survive in the city.

The T-junction at Drive-In is named for the ghostly memory of Dar es Salaam's only drive-in cinema, long razed and built over. Drive-In was one of only two ways to reach downtown from the northern part of Dar es Salaam, so it was impossible to navigate around it. The two-lane road that led to the intersection was slow moving due to speedbumps and heavy traffic, and the chaotic merging of traffic around Namanga, a corner whose commerce was a relic of earlier days of the city, but whose fruit stands and small shops were still well frequented. The road rolled past the homes of police and their families, past washing hung out to dry, past the huge new bright white American embassy with barriers and walls set back off the road, past the little plots where women grew *mchicha* (spinach) with questionable lead levels from constant exhaust exposure. Impatient drivers expanded the dusty, pot-holed shoulders into third and even fourth lanes. By the time this road dead-ended at Drive-In, the intersection was overloaded with cars transporting people to and from city center. It was just far enough on people's commute, whether home or to work, that they were in a bad mood when they got there. For many of my driving years in Dar es Salaam, I drove up to Drive-In and thought, God damn it, when are we going to get a traffic light up here? By the time I left, I no longer thought that since I had become well-versed in synchronized turning.

Synchronized turning evolved as a way of allowing the most possible vehicles to pass through an intersection against a heavy flow of oncoming traffic, in the absence of either lights or policemen to direct traffic. It took both collaboration and risk-taking. Once a large number of determined turners built up at the intersection, the driver in front bravely, persistently inched his or her vehicle into the oncoming traffic, ignoring curses and horns and flashing lights. As the lead car established takeover of the lane of oncoming traffic, a pack of cars, minivans, *bajajis*, motorcycles, bicycles, and anything else on wheels gathered behind it. At the precise moment some unlucky driver in the oncoming traffic, realizing he no longer retained possession of his lane, applied his brakes, the bolus of vehicles behind the lead car surged forward as one.

There were no specific rules, but it was helpful not to make eye contact with anyone in the line of infuriated oncoming drivers. Those of us in the swarm kept the turn alive by keeping our front bumpers no more than two inches from the previous vehicle.

The synchronized turn ended when the oncoming traffic lost patience and started laying on horns in earnest, or when a timid driver lost nerve and didn't push his or her car aggressively enough into the traffic.

I still recall the first time I was the lead car, risking the flank of my little blue Vitz to the oncoming traffic and a cacophony of horns. After I blocked the flow, a dozen or more cars, a couple of *bajajis*, and some bicyclists got through. I smiled to myself, satisfied, as I wriggled my Vitz into my spot in the lane, which was already moving forward. Who needs traffic lights, anyway?

::::: **3** :::::

# Best News I've Had All Day

**M**y head hurt. My eyes ached. I had to pee but thought I might be able to clear my inbox first, so like a bad dream, I just kept deliriously deleting. I had a protocol four weeks overdue and an all-day presentation the next day, and I had not started the slides. I had a manuscript for which I needed feedback from people in places where email didn't work. I had to figure out what to do with an intern I didn't ask for, and write an email that had to be reviewed by people on two continents before being sent to someone who had probably forgotten that she asked for it. I had spent the morning not concentrating on a meeting where earnest Canadians told Tanzanians how to reduce maternal mortality in their region, which the Canadians had never visited.

It was 3:03 p.m., which meant I either slogged through till the end of the day or left for a lunch break and worked late.

The hell with this lousy afternoon. I grabbed my keys.

It was time for a quest to fulfill my Beauty Duties. Beauty Duties included having my eyebrows threaded, various other hair removed, and keeping my toenails neat, perky, and colorful. My female Dar es Salaam friends considered Beauty Duties to be absolute musts.

They didn't need to say anything to me anymore, would just glance at my feet and give me a look. I had adapted to much of life in Tanzania, but it was hard for me to keep up with this level of beauty maintenance. Beauty Duties were not a part of my life when I lived in Vermont. In Tanzania, I couldn't get away with neglecting them. What choice do you have when your toes are always on display in sandals? This afternoon, it suited me to conform. It was the perfect reason to abandon the office and the endless emails.

My mood didn't improve on the drive to my salon. I had to roll up my window as I approached the intersection where pre-teen boys, high on glue, sloshed dirty water on windshields, squeegeed it off, and asked for money. They would start out with a begging innocent expression, then switch to a rude gesture as they let their eyes linger on my legs. One of my friends reported that a doped-up boy actually licked her windshield, completely freaking out her kids.

I was in luck—the light was green so I didn't have to stop. I darted my little car around corners, through potholes, swerved to avoid cars driving in my lane, beeped as I overtook *bajajis*. I punctuated my race car driving with curses in English and Swahili: "Turn on your directional, bitch!" "*Mshenzi!* (Asshole!)" "*We! Namna gani?* (What the hell, dude?)" Driving in Dar made me the worst person I can possibly be.

I parked, sprang out of the car, and ran for the salon to avoid the crushing heat that poured in when the air conditioning was switched off. As soon as I heard the jingle of the bells over the door, I began to feel better. Three ladies sat on a couch facing the door. They were on the tail end of a good laugh. It sounded like a good laugh about men. Or sex.

Rehema smiled, stood up, and said, "We were waiting for you." She led me behind the curtain that separated the reception from the salon.

My salon was not fancy. For a pedicure, the customer sat in the chair attached to the huge helmet-like hair dryer, careful not to bang her head, and the attendant dragged a stool over. They did not have a wide range of products, and the brands featured sometimes had labels in Chinese. Or no labels at all.

Today, two Arab women were having pedicures. They wore *bui-bui*, the black head covering and robe that reaches the floor, and chatted in Swahili with Eveline, who was doing their nails. A man delivering food in foil containers stuck his head behind the curtain and they adjusted their hijabs so that only their eyes were visible.

I heard my name joyfully shouted. Lily, who does my hair, rushed over with shining eyes and put her arms around my shoulders. She leaned her head in to mine and whispered "*Nimeenda.* (I went.)"

I gasped and threw my arms around her. I was surprised, and I was happy. "How was it?" I asked. "How did it go? What happened?"

Lily just laughed and told me that it had gone great. And that it had been free, just like I told her.

Lily, a single mother supporting a family of three, had told me her story over a year earlier, while she was putting highlights in my hair. When she was pregnant five years earlier, she went to the private clinic of a highly-respected obstetrician, one of the old generation who held a professorship and had taught many of the doctors in Tanzania. As most doctors in Tanzania do, he worked in the public sector, but earned money through his private practice. Many doctors only go to work in the government health facilities to refer clients to their private practice.

Lily's famous doctor did not show up for her birth, during which she got an extensive tear that damaged the skin around her perineum. That fistula caused her to leak urine. When she went to the same doctor a few weeks after the birth, he told her that she would need to pay the equivalent of $400 for him to do the surgery to repair the fistula, the equivalent of over three months of her salary. There was no way she could afford it.

I knew what she could do, and where she could go. A hospital in Dar es Salaam did fistula repairs for free, and had a good reputation for treating their clients with respect and kindness.

For over a year, I tried to get Lily to go to this hospital. I set up appointments, found phone numbers, strategized about what she could tell them at the reception desk, reminded, followed up gently... until I gave up. At some point, I understood this was my answer to Lily's life situation, not hers. Sometimes the intensity at which you push is equal to the lagging of the person being pushed. Lily wasn't ready to go to that hospital when I was trying to make that happen.

I don't know what changed for Lily. But she went (*nimeenda!*) and both of our lives were changed. Mine, only for an afternoon. My black mood was transformed into an electric lilac ether of joyfulness, which coincided with the color I chose for my toe nails. Hers, an end to almost five years of discomfort.

I had to face the congested and angst-filled road to go back to the office, the emails, the unwanted intern, the meetings, and the earnest Canadians, but I went with a smile on my face. It was an afternoon where Lily's story and mine intersected with a happy outcome.

::::::: **4** :::::::

# Dar Now and Then

I came to Tanzania for the first time in 1992, with nothing more than a postcard from my friend Dan, inviting me to help him with his research project in Tanga. To get to Tanga I had to first fly into Dar es Salaam, and that was when I first met that town.

I stayed at the YWCA, right off of Posta, along with Peace Corps volunteers, who periodically came to Dar from their villages on their days off, and other low-budget travelers. There was a 10 p.m. curfew and a simple cafeteria. Men and women stayed in separate parts of the building. To make a phone call, I had to go to the Telecom Center on Samora Avenue and stand in line for a booth. An operator would connect me with my number, and I would have a few precious and carefully metered minutes of communication with my parents.

I did not understand Dar right away. After Liberia, Sierra Leone, and Ivory Coast, I walked around town asking myself, where is the color? Whitewashed walls were dingy and beige or faded and white. There were fewer people than in Monrovia, Freetown, or Abidjan, and there were no women wearing the fabulous colors and towering headpieces I saw in those cities. As my eyes and heart adjusted to the muted tones of the city and its people, I started to love it. I learned to speak Swahili and delighted in the double meanings and insinuations in the language, the tendency to convey meanings in clever ways. I came to understand that what I perceived as a lack of vigor was in fact subtlety and politeness. Dar es Salaam had an innocence in its lack of urban hustle. The expanses of palm-tree-framed beaches with turquoise waters helped too.

In Dar, there were only a half dozen or so places for me to go when my friends and I wanted a night out, but that was enough, and I always knew at least a quarter of the crowd. Under the massive mango tree in the courtyard of Palm Beach Hotel, we kick-started the evening with a beer before heading downtown to the night-club Bilicana's. On the drive along Ocean Road's curves, the ocean crashed against black craggy cliffs that melted into an expanse of sand, with thickets of cacti clinging to the black rock. The water was beautifully turquoise during the day and purple-black at night, often dotted on the horizon with the lights of ships waiting to unload their cargo in the port.

For a mellow night, I would hang with my friends at Miami's, a local outdoor drinking spot off an unpaved road in Masaki. We sat in plastic chairs, swatted mosquitoes, and drank beer, or maybe a Coke with *konyagi*, or we sat at the bar made out of a converted shipping container. Late at night, we would find a taxi and pile in, drunk, sober, giggly young women, and ride home with the windows down, arriving not only safely but often with a new friend in the taxi driver. On really late nights that turned into early mornings, we would see the fishermen disembarking their local boats with their night's catch. They spilled noisily out of their boats, their shouting and roughness dispelling romantic notions inspired by their serene silhouettes on the water's horizon moments before.

Back then, the drive from downtown to Mikocheni only took a few minutes, and along the way we encountered only a few vehicles.

By 2015, this drive took up to three hours during rush hour, where the queue of traffic snaked on like a glittery conga line. Mbezi, now Dar's middle-class bedroom community, was considered a wild frontier in the '90s; only a few brave and crazy souls lived like home-steaders on massive plots. There were so few cars that we identified people by what they drove, as in "so-and-so, you know, he drives the Land Cruiser short chassis." My husband-to-be, Medzio, was one of a handful of people who owned a motorcycle with an engine larger than 125 cc. In fact, he met his best friend, Renatus Ideka, because they both had big bikes. They kept seeing each other on the streets, and one day Renatus flagged Medzio down to introduce himself as the other man in Dar es Salaam with a 250-cc bike. Both of them were in the habit of outriding the traffic policemen, who only had 125-cc engines.

Once Medzio was idling at a traffic light and a traffic policeman he had left in the dust several times snuck up behind him on foot and yanked the keys out of his ignition with a triumphant, "I've got you now!"

At the station, the cop realized that not only was Medzio's father from the same tribe as him, he was also the cop's wife's obstetrician. From then on, the cop was a friendly cop, and that friendship proved useful some years later, when Medzio was driving me to the National Institute of Medical Research on the same motorcycle and a Land Cruiser pulled out in front of him. We hit it head-on. Medzio, who wore a full helmet, flew over the top of the motorcycle and crashed face-first into the vehicle.

I had to pull myself out from under the bike and drag Medzio, unconscious, to the side of the road, at which point the friendly cop appeared and took charge. He flagged down a passing pickup truck to take us to Muhimbili Hospital, and Medzio's bike was taken to the police station for safekeeping. The pickup dropped us at the maternity ward, where Medzio's father emerged from the surgical theater, sized up the wounds on Medzio's head, stitched up his son's face, and took us home.

None of this would happen in today's Dar es Salaam: the vehicles people bonded over, the friendship with the policeman, the assistance in an accident, the ride to Muhimbili, locating a doctor at the nation's largest national referral hospital when no one had a cell phone.

Even the crime seemed innocent in those days in Dar. Watch out for pickpockets, I was told. Don't change money on the black market. Ladies of the night were available, at SkyWay for the more upmarket customer, or on the streets of Oyster Bay for a less expensive adventure. Cheapest of all were the women you could have for almost nothing in the Kinondoni graveyard. People were more worried about catching gonorrhea than HIV.

Tanzania began its shift from socialism to open market economy in the early '90s. Off the heels of socialism, scarcity was the norm. Blue Band margarine, canned Zesta jam, and local flour packaged in paper packs were the only things you could count on to be on the store shelves. Vegetables were plentiful, however, at the TX market in Kinondoni. When everyone was poor, no one wanted what he or she couldn't have. The increase in goods happened in parallel with tremendous urban shift, as hundreds of thousands of Tanzanians from rural areas came to Dar to look for employment, a life beyond subsistence agriculture. From 1992 to 2012, Dar changed from 1.4 million to 4.4 million people. The tone and tempo of life in Dar changed drastically as well.

By 2015, Dar was no longer the sweet town I had known. In my last year there, we saw our Malawian friends and employees rounded up by the police and beset by thugs who took advantage of their vulnerability. Three were killed trying to stop people from looting their homes. One woman was gang-raped and killed when men broke into her home. Our neighbor's gardener came to work with cuts and bruises from fending off looters, only managing to survive because some neighbors helped him out. A friend was hijacked from the airport by four men in a taxi and taken from ATM to ATM to withdraw money and then left by the side of the road. Every day, pedestrians had cars drive up to them and thieves snatch whatever they were carrying, dragging them along in the process, injuring, and in one case, killing them.

Another friend woke up to bloodcurdling screams in the middle of the night to find that a *boda boda* driver had been attacked with a knife by his two passengers as they tried to steal his motorcycle in the dark street in front of her house. When he tossed the keys into the bushes they ran away.

A Tanzanian friend who lived in *uswazi*—slang for where the locals live, in rented rooms with communal cooking spaces and toilets—described how she had to befriend local drug addicts to try to have peace of mind about the safety of her ten-year-old daughter. Her daughter had to wear ear plugs to do homework because of the noise from the local drinking spot next door, with sex and music and fights lasting long into the night.

For months, I drove the long way home to avoid an intersection where boys jacked up on glue aggressively slopped water on my windshield. Sometimes they begged for money, sometimes they made lewd gestures, sometimes both. A friend had her windshield wipers broken by one of these kids when she said she didn't want her window washed. I avoided the intersection because it provoked such contradictory and unkind feelings in me: Sometimes I looked at the boys barely older than my sons and felt so sorry for them, and sometimes I hated them.

The stories go on and on: dogs poisoned, guards murdered,

window grills forced open with car jacks. In the '90s, people started building walls around compounds. First, the walls had broken bottles stuck into the cement as a deterrent to would-be invaders. Next came barbed wire, and now high-voltage electric wire can be seen on many of the walls. Where there used to be one private security company, there are now a dozen.

I came home from the airport late one night when, at a very busy and dangerous intersection, the door of a car stopped next to us opened and a young man was pushed out. He wove his way unsteadily through the traffic and collapsed next to the side of the road. He started sobbing, wailing, crying as if his life was ruined, his knees pulled up to his chest and his head in his arms. His sobs of utter desolation tore at me, and I looked at my Tanzanian companions in the car—but they just shrugged and said it was probably a scam.

The roads became so congested that we had to leave the house at 6:00 a.m. to get the kids to school before the 6:15 traffic jam started. My Tanzanian friends who lived farther out left home at 5:00 or earlier.

Traffic jams became the norm of life in Dar, as did crazy, lawless, every-driver-for-himself driving. Dar es Salaam traffic activated a Mr. Hyde part of my personality. I cursed, I refused to let buses take over my lane, I played chicken with *dala-dalas*, I honked when the car in front of me drove too slowly, I cut cars off, ran red lights after dark. I left people standing by the zebra crossing instead of letting them cross the road, since I knew that I would be rear-ended if I stopped.

Years earlier, I bragged to my Nairobi friends that in Dar, I could drive with the windows down at any time of the day or night. That became a thing of the past after a guy reached in my rolled-down window and ripped an earring out of my ear at 6:30 in the morning while I waited at a traffic light. A few weeks later, a crazy person threw feces wrapped in paper at the car while I drove the kids to school in the morning. It hit the back passenger side window, at eye level with one of the kids.

The social net of Dar es Salaam ripped over time. Too many people, too much hustle, too many cars, and too much garbage. Too many luxury goods to steal, too many people trying to make a quick buck. Corruption, crime, and greed became integrated into life, and I had a hard time seeing the way back. When I accepted Tanzania as my other home, I accepted that my kids would not have some of the things I encountered as a child that made me essentially me: the smell of a pine forest, summer nights light till 9 p.m., playing in the snow till your fingers grew numb. But I always assumed that I traded those wonderful missed opportunities of life in the United States for the wonderful found opportunities of living in Tanzania. My realization of the depths to which Dar es Salaam had plunged were most raw and shocking when I thought about the kids who were inheriting this increasingly crime-ridden city: my kids, my friends', and all the other children growing up in Dar es Salaam.

Ugliness, urban blight, crime exist everywhere in our world. But in Africa, it is very much in-your-face. It is not filtered by a functioning police system, homeless shelters where street children can go, a functional solid waste disposal system. Instead, the plastic bags and young kids with lean faces and women selling their bodies are all right there.

When I realized that the soundest choice for insulating myself and my family from this disturbing reality was to put up our car window, I started thinking about moving back to the U.S.

# Traditional Greetings Among Wazungu and Watanzania

**⚥⚥ Advice to Wazungu:** When you greet your Tanzanian friend, he will grasp your hand and lean his shoulder into each of your shoulders, in turn. Expect it, since his shoulder will end up in your windpipe if you don't. Your Tanzanian friend will keep hold of your hand after shaking it, and may hold it throughout your conversation. If you walk down the street with a friend, expect to walk very slowly. When two men are strolling down the street holding hands, it means that they are friends.

**⚥⚥ Advice to Watanzania:** *Wazungu* come from different places, including Europe, America, and these days, South America. Traditionally, Americans hug when greeting and Europeans kiss cheeks. When you greet your American friend, expect a hug in which he or she will squeeze your upper body quite tightly, but only once. Your American friend might start hugging you as a greeting and a farewell the very first time you meet him or her.

# Upcountry

::::::: **5** :::::::

# Peace Like a Monkey

The three weeks we owned a vervet monkey were lovely, amazing, emotional, and stressful. She came into our lives because of me: my mother's guilt; my love of Tanzania's freedom and wildness; my optimism that everything would turn out for the best. She was an animal alter ego to my impulsiveness.

I was doing fieldwork on a study of maternal health in the Tanga region. The dates fell on my younger son's third birthday, and I felt tremendously guilty about missing it. My dear friend Asma Ramadhan Khamis, a midwife from Zanzibar, called me from a health center in Tanga. She had helped resuscitate a newborn and the family had offered her a gift: a vervet monkey. Would I like to bring it to my son as a birthday gift?

So there I was, nervous and bemused, driving up to the health center an hour away where Asma was working to see this monkey. This wasn't a good idea, I knew, but I thought, I'll just look.

I met two guys with the monkey just outside of the health center. They had tied the monkey's hands and feet together with surgical gauze in preparation for handing her over to me. She was docile yet alert, did not protest the untying of the hands, her eyes bold and quick but not angry. She was smaller than I had expected, graceful, not needy but receptive to me. She let me stroke her fur and gave me sideways glances with her light brown eyes.

I had those guys put the monkey into a box and put it in the rear of my company vehicle. Although my driver said nothing, I could tell by his anxious glances in the rearview mirror that he was wondering whether the monkey confined in a cardboard box would escape and jump on him. I ignored his sulky expression as I pondered what I would do with the monkey for the two days before we headed back to Dar. Could I tie her up in my room in the guest house? Could I tie her to a tree outside without her being tormented by children?

Back at my rural dispensary, the nurses and I weighed the options. I vetoed the idea of strapping the monkey's box to the back of a rented motorbike to take her to the community livestock officer's house. The next idea was to ask the village chairman. However, he was at a critical time with local elections. Would he come?

To my immense relief, the village chairman was able to pry himself away from election proceedings to deal with the pressing monkey accommodation situation that had sprung up within his constituency. His name was Mr. Matata, which means "problem" in Kiswahili, but he was anything but for me and, in short order, an arrangement had been made. The monkey was to stay with Matata himself.

Two days went by as we wrapped up our work assessing the quality of maternal health care in the dispensary in Kabuku.

When it was time to leave for home, I stopped by Mr. Matata's house, where the monkey was tied with a sisal rope around her waist to a post in a mud hut. A constellation of excited children gathered by the door to catch a glimpse of her. She held still to let me stroke her fur. She seemed … sad. I had spent the last two days trying to convince myself that this was not actually going to be a disaster. Seeing her boosted my sense of righteousness. See, I thought to myself, she's a beautiful creature, and clearly so easy to take care of. Even a person with only a mud hut and no particular monkey-care accessories can do it, and certainly we can too.

To get her to our home in Dar es Salaam, she would have to be packed back in the cardboard box. I realized, as our car pulled up in front of Mr. Matata's house, that I had not thought through how this would happen.

Mr. Matata made some half-hearted attempts to grab her and she bared her sharp incisors and slapped at him. Even though he had been an enthusiastic host to the monkey, he was not willing to risk his well-being to stuff her back into the cardboard box. I realized that I was the one who had to do it. I was afraid of a nasty monkey bite, but it was I who created this situation and I had to resolve it. The driver and a team of colleagues waited in the car for me to pick up the monkey so that we could go home after two weeks of fieldwork. I had to do this now.

I took a deep breath, grabbed her by the scruff of the neck, and to the sound of new and scary monkey vocalizations, crammed her in the box. Mr. Matata tied the box with some plant fibers, put it in the back of the car, and plunked a burlap sack of beans on top so she wouldn't be able to escape. I got in the car with my heart hammering, smiled sweetly at my colleagues, and said, "*Twende.* (Let's go.)"

I was on the way home when a text message came in from Andrew Perkin, my biologist friend, whom I had consulted by text a couple of days ago: "Don't do it," he wrote. "Major problems."

To distract myself from a sinking feeling that this decision was massive folly, I focused on picking a name for the monkey. I decided to call her Teule after a hospital in the Tanga region. Later, when I asked my husband what Teule meant in Kiswahili, he said, "I don't know, glory or something...very churchy." I found out from a colleague that it means "chosen one."

When we reached home, the boys ran out to the car to meet me. Sheer joy emanated from Janusz and Tadzio when Teule unfurled herself from the box, leaving me to wonder, how *did* I get her into that box in the first place? They did everything I thought was a bad idea: grabbed her, shook her hand, stuck their faces in hers. I hovered nearby, feeling both very nervous and very proud and whispering unheeded commands to the boys. We tied Teule's leash to a tree and she climbed up onto the roof, where she stayed for quite some time before descending for some fruit we offered to her.

The next morning at daybreak, I was jolted awake by an ungodly cacophony. I knew what it was before my eyelids even opened. I sprinted outside to where Teule's leash was tied to the tree. It was the crows. Dar es Salaam was a city under siege. We lived with a plague of crows: crows that killed songbirds; crows that stole items from tables; crows that took food from babies. These highly intelligent creatures worked as a pack, and about thirty circled Teule, creating a horrible audio assault on the cowering monkey. Upon seeing me, she sheepishly came down the tree while I tried unsuccessfully to nail the bastards with rocks. I was flooded with affection and relief that she was OK, as well as a newfound protectiveness.

Teule and our family got to know each other. We sat on the couch with our backs to her until she came closer to us and touched us.

*Janusz's morning smile with Teule.*

Eventually I ran my fingers through her fur. She made a chittering sound. Then she groomed me in return, picking imaginary bugs and pieces of lint off my pajamas with her fingers and mouth. I groomed her stomach, and she rolled over onto her back and threw one arm in the air, a picture of total submission.

We learned that she loved cucumbers and corn, and she wouldn't eat a banana unless she peeled it herself. She made a lovely sound like a horse whinnying whenever she saw one of the four of us. She carefully watched all of our comings and goings, both in and out of the house. When one of us left, she climbed to the highest point to see exactly where we went. I have never felt so *kept track of*. I noticed that, although Medzio still held that adopting her had been a bad idea, he was often the one taking her pieces of fruit.

I had to hand it to a fellow primate, she was an astute observer of social hierarchy. She knew who was the core family and where her loyalties lay. She and Janusz bonded right away, and if he woke up early, he could be found on the back porch with Teule. My husband, in a very manly fashion, found practical ways to express

*Marya, Tadzio and Teule sit on the back porch enjoying the sunshine.*

his fondness for her. He attached a carabiner to her leash to extend the area she could roam. I looked forward to the time in the morning when I would sit out on the back porch with her and groom her before anyone else woke up, rewarded by her chittering noise. Whoever thought that having a monkey would be so peaceful?

The sand started shifting out from under my feet as we discovered Teule's dislikes. Rough-housing was one of them. One time when our nanny was chasing our son, Teule took a mighty swipe at her, drawing blood. She bit a ten-year-old friend of ours, thankfully not breaking the skin. She made aggressive advances at the gardener. My biologist friend's text message echoed in my mind: *Don't do it. Major problems.*

We lengthened her leash and with the carabiner on it, she could move to various parts of the yard. This often resulted in her getting tangled up in tree branches and one of the adults in the house had to climb up and untangle her. I canceled playdates for Janusz because I wanted to avoid liability issues. Like parents of a wayward child, we were spending all of our time and energy trying to manage Teule's behavior. In a dreadful though ultimately successful session, a brave veterinarian armed only with a towel managed to give Teule her tetanus shot. I acted as a matador while he jabbed. He then told me in no uncertain terms thawt not only was it illegal to keep the monkey as a pet, I would be fully responsible should anyone be injured by her.

The boys weren't old enough to take responsibility, I was away at work all day, and Medzio hadn't asked for all this additional work. And now, the well-being and future of this endearing creature was my responsibility—and obsession. This little monkey was taking over my life.

After the fifth time Medzio had to borrow a ladder to get Teule untangled from a tree, I came home from work to find a black cloud over the household. Although he kindly refrained from saying, "I told you so," it was obvious that we were in over our heads, and that Teule would have to go.

From a friend, I got the phone number of a veterinarian who passed me along to a South African woman who had experience releasing vervets. When I got off the phone with her, I informed the family that she was coming to pick up Teule the next day.

Although my first reaction to Teule's new twist of fate was enormous relief, a painful sense of melancholy settled firmly in my stomach. She would be gone. She could be harmed, or killed even, by wild vervets. We would never see her again.

The morning that Teule was to go, we awoke to find that she had gotten tangled in some branches on the roof. Before I could say no, Janusz said, "I'll get her, Mama!" and climbed up a tree, onto the roof, and untangled the monkey. At one point, Teule started bobbing her head aggressively (she hated it when anyone put pressure on the leash) and I almost shouted at him to stop. As I watched him, I was filled with pride. Janusz at seven, displaying two things I love so much about him: fearlessness and compassion.

For the whole day, my heart was in my stomach. I couldn't avoid thinking of Teule in the box, of her being broken away from the impromptu troupe we had become, of how empty the garden would feel without her. Earlier that week, I had met with a good friend of mine who was having man troubles and thinking of breaking up with her boyfriend of several years. She spoke about it coolly, while my heart started beating faster as I thought of parting with the monkey. What is wrong with me? I wondered. Am I such an addict for taking care of souls that I can't divest myself of one small primate, despite the fact that it so clearly is not working out?

The South African woman came and took her away, to be released to the wild, where her chances of survival were fifty-fifty.

The garden indeed felt empty for weeks as we remembered Teule.

Two months later, we visited the United States on vacation. A man behind us on a bus chatted with my boys. When the conversation turned to pets, they informed him that they had had a monkey. He chuckled, "You did, huh?" clearly thinking he was humoring imaginative children. Yes, they did, I thought back, in a proud, strong tone. Yes, we live in Africa, and they have an impulsive, imperfect working mother who sometimes makes crazy, impractical decisions. But for a gem of a few weeks, we had a monkey. And we'll never forget it.

## ⁞⁞⁞⁞⁞ 6 ⁞⁞⁞⁞⁞
# Tanga Road Story

I dozed for the first part of the trip, mesmerized by the rhythm of the road as we left Tanga, the sisal fields stretching off into the distance on our left side, green spikes against the blue sky, rooted to red soil. It had been a busy trip, visiting Bombo Hospital and several health facilities to talk to health care providers about how to provide routine HIV testing.

I was traveling with Lusekelo Njonge, a medical doctor, and Rehema Athumani, as well as the driver, Caroli.* Lusekelo was the newest member of my monitoring and evaluation team. Previously, he had served as a district medical officer responsible for Simanjiro district in the Manyara region. Rehema Athumani was a soft-spoken young woman who worked as an administrative assistant for the program. The driver, Caroli, wore sunglasses all the time, had a gravelly enthusiastic voice, a chronically hungry look, and a propensity to speed.

The days we spent in Tanga wouldn't fix the problems, but I was hopeful that by looking over shoulders and convincing managers and health care providers of the importance of HIV testing, we made a difference. A job well done? The job is never done, but well enough for me to doze off in the car on the five-hour drive back to Dar, where our families waited for us. The car slowed and the change in speed pulled me from my drowsy reverie. I looked out the window to see what Caroli reacted to. A crowd of people appeared up ahead of us on the right side of the road. To the left and right sides of the road, I saw simple one-room houses made of mud and sticks and concrete, a couple with metal roofs and the rest with thatch. A corn field with dried-looking husks waited for the harvest. An unpaved road joined the main road at a ninety-degree angle, and it was there that a crowd was gathered. Two men stepped into the road and waved branches at us, the universal African signal to stop. I leaned towards the window to see what the crowd concealed, but couldn't get a view. The men and women looked like the people you expect to meet in a rural Tanzanian village on a farming work day. They wore battered and dusty work clothes, had calloused hands and worn faces. Some of them turned around to track our car with their eyes as we passed. Among them, I saw one woman in a faded *kanga*. She knelt on the ground and did not look up as we passed.

In Tanzania, you never stop a car for a crowd, to avoid robberies and carjacking. See crowd, keep moving, don't make eye contact. That's the rule. So while all of us peered out the window to see what was going on, Caroli behind his reflective shades calculated how to carry us by as quickly as possible while not hitting any of the people begging us to stop.

The crowd faded behind us as we crested a little hill. I turned to Lusekelo as he turned to me and we looked each other in the eyes for another second. "Stop the car," I said to Caroli. Rehema exhaled. I could tell from the quickness with which Caroli applied the brakes and steered the car towards a habitable patch of corn stubble that he also approved.

All four of us got out of the car and walked together back towards the crowd, our feet crunching grasses and corn stalks. I looked over at Lusekelo and saw that he was carrying a first aid kit from the car. As we approached the crowd, several people came towards us. The grandfatherly-looking man who had been waving the branch trotted up to us and grasped Lusekelo's hand first, then mine. He had a deeply lined face, and his eyes were filled with concern.

He walked us briskly to the center of the gathering, by a little dip in the dirt road, his rough hand still enfolding mine. The kneeling woman had not moved. Now I saw a piece of grass clinging to the back of her head, and the braids which held her hair were several days old. The kanga wrapped around her shoulders was worn, it was transparent in places. She was quietly keening, a sound that hadn't penetrated the car window as we rolled past.

In front of her, a boy was stretched out in the grass. Someone had tucked a prayer mat under him, and he lay mostly on it. His eyes were closed and from time-to-time he would lift his arm and drop it again and when he did he moaned and shook his head.

The man holding my hand introduced himself as the boy's uncle. He told me that a few hours ago, Hamid had been in the field with his mother and himself when Hamid's mother asked him to go tell his sister to start preparing a meal for the evening. Hamid wanted to use his uncle's bicycle to go back to the house, but his mother was concerned that he might damage the bicycle. His uncle said it was OK, and Hamid, who was ten years old, flushed with pleasure and took off on the bike. It was too tall for him to sit on, so he stood on the pedals. His mother and uncle watched him go, the bike swaying back and forth. They shook their heads and smiled and raised their hoes again.

About forty minutes later, one of the neighbor's children ran out to the field to say that Hamid had been knocked off the bicycle by a tractor driver. The tractor, traveling at high speed, didn't stop. Hamid's leg was pinned between the bicycle and the tractor wheel and had snapped like a twig.

I watched Hamid's mother brushed an ant off of his face. Her body was rigid with distress. Salt from tears had left streaks of fine-grained glitter on Hamid's dark brown skin. It was hard to tell if he was unconscious or exhausted.

Lusekelo gathered details from Hamid's uncle. The time of the accident? Roughly three hours prior. They had been trying to flag down a vehicle for the past two hours or so, but no one had stopped. The location of the nearest police station? About thirty kilometers away, in a town called Mkata. The nearest hospital? Also Mkata.

He kneeled beside the mother, greeting her gently, asking her some questions. She put her hand on her son's shoulder and roused him with a little shake. Lusekelo spoke to Hamid, touched his arm, and finally turned his attention to the boy's leg. Hamid raised himself to his elbows and protested as Lusekelo touched his leg. His pleas intensified as Lusekelo put his hands on the leg and examined the break. Once he moved as if to remove Lusekelo's hands, but his uncle growled a warning to the boy and he did not do it again.

Hamid's uncle lifted the woman up by her shoulders and led her away. I could see her shaky movements, and imagined how much she wanted to go back to her son's side. Janusz, my own ten-year-old boy, was safe in our house in Dar es Salaam. Please let him be safe, I prayed. Please let Hamid be OK.

Lusekelo gave orders to the men around him. One man trotted up with a sturdy, smooth stick about a meter long which he brought to Lusekelo. Another man stripped the inner tube from the tire of the bicycle, while a third produced a *panga* to cut the inner tube.

When Lusekelo set the boy's leg, forcing the leg with its shattered bone to lie straight against the stick and tying it with the inner tube, Hamid's screams ran through us. Straight through us, like a knife. The mothers shuddered and gaped, some women reaching for their hair, some covering their mouths. The men stood stone-faced around the boy, with Lusekelo and another man wrapping, pressing, straightening, tying his leg. His mother cried as if struck as he screamed for her over and over, his voice becoming more frantic, desperate and shrill and then hopeless and trailed with sobs. My blood turned to ice. Dear God. Had I ever felt more horrified, more helpless?

The next hour passed quickly, since there were things to do. Caroli drove to the police station and brought back a policewoman to write an accident report, which would be necessary for Hamid to get treatment at the hospital. Rehema took up a collection, to which we contributed the greatest amount. Lusekelo insisted that the boy needed to go to the referral hospital, Tumbi, rather than the closer district hospital, because of the severity of the break. However, this was a two-hour ride. The policewoman, uncharacteristically helpful, stopped a *dala-dala* and insisted that they take the boy and his family to Tumbi and helped negotiate a price for the necessary seats. Hamid's mother and his uncle got into the vehicle and Hamid was lifted into the *dala-dala,* his pain evident.

After the *dala-dala* left, we said our goodbyes so as to get back on the road, thinking of our families back in Dar es Salaam. Gratitude glowed in the eyes of the men and women who grasped our hands, especially as they thanked Lusekelo. It humbled me. I thought about how it must feel to try to flag down cars for hours while your nephew, son, neighbor was unconscious, all of the cars slowing down only enough to gawk and then speed up, eyes deliberately avoiding contact. If we hadn't stopped, would anyone have stopped? Would Hamid still be lying in the grass? Would he be alive the next morning?

We all worked together for years. Lusekelo eventually took another job, Rehema moved to another project, and Caroli was fired for financial misconduct. But we always had a special smile for each other, an unspoken memory of that moment when we all breathed out the same thought: stop the car.

---

*Not his real name.

::::::  **7**  ::::::

# The Making (and Breaking) of Rules Regarding Toilets

The second cup of Africafe was my first mistake.

I generally abstain from coffee if what is on offer has either "powdered" or "granulated" in its description. But that morning my eyes were scratchy from a sleepless night in a decrepit hotel. I kept flashing back to the hard foam pillow with the frilly pink sateen cover, the cursed AC that did nothing more than wheeze tepid air, and the musty smell of soggy carpet adjacent to the bathroom. The whine of mosquitoes still rang in my ears as I stirred myself up one cup, and then another. It was time to get on with my day.

My second mistake I attribute to exhaustion: I broke my APWYC rule. The APWYC rule came from time spent in New York City and in Africa. The rule is "Always Pee When You Can." Whether in New York or Africa, you should always treat the chance to pee with dignity or hygiene as an opportunity not to pass up. APWYC.

I started to feel that second cup of coffee as our car bumped its way over the gravelly road on the way to the hospital. My colleagues and I were on the way to Korogwe District Hospital to evaluate the site for a study on routine HIV testing in outpatient departments. We arrived, shook hands with hospital staff, exchanged warm greetings, and we all sat down to discuss the study. Pens emerged, notepads blossomed, the atmosphere turned earnest, the discussions began.

And then it hit me. I had to pee. Really, really had to pee.

I am a scientist, and at that moment I was a scientist with a pen and paper in my hand, who had to pee. I sketched out my situation analysis on my pad and it looked like this:

**Pee Potential Analysis, Phase I: Preparation**

| Element | Key Considerations | Status |
| --- | --- | --- |
| Toilet tissue | Check. Wearing same pants as yesterday and I remembered to stuff tissue in the pocket. | Ready to go. |
| Awareness of location | Negative. Have not visited this facility before. Will have to discretely interrupt proceedings to ask a female staff member of the location. | Find the right moment. Do it in Kiswahili so American Principal Investigator (PI) does not understand. |
| Physical assessment | Poor. Knees still swollen after foolish decision to play soccer two weeks ago. | Will have to tough it out. |
| Timing | Imminent. Situation does not allow for waiting for earnest introduction to be over. | Let's do this thing. |

The PI from the United States was deep in her convincing and passionate introduction related to the inordinate challenges of HIV testing in the outpatient department, when I discretely pulled my chair back. I walked over to the most bored-looking woman in the room and whispered my request in her ear. She nodded her head briskly, and we walked to the door. The PI didn't appear to notice, but many of my Tanzanian colleagues sent longing glances as we exited the room.

My guide turned out to be in charge of the maternity ward, which was not where our study would be conducted. That morning, she was called upon to meet the visitors so that the welcoming committee did not look thin. She left me by a wooden door, which I entered to find a latrine-style squat toilet. I moved on to the second stage of situational analysis.

## Pee Potential Analysis Stage II: Premises Assessment

| Element | Key Considerations | Status |
|---------|-------------------|--------|
| Running water | Negative. Battered orange Omo bucket and cut off water bottle, no water whatsoever. Realize I left my alcohol hand rub in backpack, front pocket. | Situation less than optimal. Will have to proceed without water OR wipe. |
| Illumination | Very poor. Dim outlines visible by light of very small window covered by a tattered curtain. | Manageable. Don't really want to see my surroundings anyway. |
| Hygiene/smell | Abysmal. No description needed. This is perhaps the lowest tier of toilet in the world, a public toilet in a government hospital in Africa. | I'm ready. I broke my APWYC rule and brought this on myself. |
| Space and dimensions | Tricky. Only one wall nearby to support myself since I cannot go into a full squat with the bad knees. | Adopt yoga chair position for the pee. |

I prepared my pants, carefully pulling up the bottoms so that they were well away from contact with the floor, pulled down the waist, and positioned myself in my yogic pee pose over the toilet when I heard the sound.

*Thwack!* The sound of something flat and metallic hitting something hard and wet.

My brain told me: I know that sound, I *know* that sound. It was the sound of my new phone hitting the porcelain surface of the toilet.

Yoga chair pose turned into a combination of down dog and triangle pose as I reached for the phone, hindered by pants around ankles.

The phone had landed on the slick, gently inclined surface of the squat toilet. For a moment I hoped, maybe it won't slip down into the gaping hole of refuse. Then I gasped as the phone began to move. It slid down and to the left. I feinted left but then the phone rode the incline of the porcelain, turned and glided to the right. Left, turn, right, turn, as gracefully as a luge team in the Winter Olympics, the phone gained momentum down the slick white slope.

*Plop!* The phone came to rest in the brackish abyss in the hole at the bottom of the toilet. But in my mind, it wasn't over. I was a nanosecond behind, but like the losing luge team, I still believed I could win this thing. I had half a second to reach into the toilet muck and grab the phone, which bobbed up and down as if to say, "I'm here! I still belong to you!"

I did it. I plunged my hand fearlessly, mindlessly into the muck of Korogwe District hospital's public toilet and grabbed my phone. I dropped it on the concrete floor. And there, in the middle of the humid, stuffy air of the toilet, an icy shiver of disgust gripped me. An involuntary sound escaped my lips. I stared at my dripping hand and wondered how many times I will have to wash it before I can ever eat with it again, or if I will just have to cut it off. I divided my little bit of toilet tissue between my hand and the phone, squinted at both in the dim light for overt signs of damage, gangrene, or giant supersized multi-drug resistant bacteria, re-dressed myself one-handed, rubbed away a few tears with my left elbow, and attempted to carry the phone out of the toilet without touching it.

I burst out of the toilet, stumbled on a short step and almost knocked down my friend and colleague Gilly Arthur. She was concerned when I didn't return to the meeting and had come to check on me. Tears smudged on my cheeks and I squinted like a mole as my eyes tried to adjust to the light of day. I held the phone between my thumb and forefinger in front of me, and tried not to look at it. I had not yet regained the power of speech. I tried to explain the situation to Gilly using hand gestures. My stifled sobs apparently looked to her as if I wanted to vomit, and she rushed me over to a nearby sink. Thankfully, it had running water. I turned it on and plunged my hand into it as a smith plunges his hot iron into a bucket.

I was shaking. No longer the cool and experienced researcher, I was wild-eyed and speechless with an erratic heartbeat, my hand under running water as I continued to flash back to that moment when my hand plunged into the toilet muck.

I divulged my secret only to Gilly and I never used that phone again.

Some rules are made to be broken, others to live by. Always Pee When You Can, sisters.

:::::: **8** ::::::

# Got Placentas?

I approached the table with trepidation disguised as indifference. A dozen Zanzibari nurses and midwives watched me step towards the surgical table with scissors in my hand.

My job: to touch, no, in fact, to pick up, handle, turn over, fiddle around with, look closely at (including putting in close proximity to my face), and possibly (if I did remember to breathe) to catch a scent of a placenta.

I was supposed to locate the place where the umbilical cord joined the placenta, turn the placenta over to the maternal side, make an incision with the scissors, and use a pipette to siphon up a few drops of blood. All with a dozen midwives watching my every move, and an American ob-gyn filming me on her iPhone, with potential for putting it up on YouTube that evening when she got back to the hotel room, for all I know.

I was the principal investigator on a study on malaria in pregnancy. Specifically, we were measuring placental malaria infection among Zanzibari women who had not had any preventative drugs for malaria during their pregnancies. I was in charge of training midwives about the study design and research ethics, as well as how to collect the blood samples. Two clinicians, Veronica Ades, ob-gyn from Manhattan via Uganda, and my dear friend, Asma Ramadhan Khamis, famous midwife and advisor to the Ministry of Health in Zanzibar, taught the midwives how to create specimens. They thought that it would be good for morale if I showed that I could create a specimen, too.

Easy for them to volunteer me. How many placentas did these midwives and obstetricians sling around a day? Easily five, seven? Ten? Me, on the other hand, well, I'll be honest. This was my first time handling a placenta.

I had worked myself up to this moment for quite some time. As a researcher, I always tried to observe the service under review. Cervical cancer screening, labor and delivery, newborn resuscitation—you name it, I've seen it.

All fine until that time I passed out in Iringa Regional Hospital, watching a circumcision procedure. I regained consciousness on the floor of the waiting room, where two dozen horrified young men and a few grandmothers had just witnessed me bursting out of the surgical theater wearing full surgical scrubs and fainting cold. Since then, I had had a hard time getting my groove back in the operating room or labor ward. My mind seemed to have very clear rules about what I could observe and remain conscious. Blood and childbirth, OK, but blood and scalpels, not. And when my mind made that "lights out!" judgment call, that was just it. Forget the advice to "breathe deeply" or "envision gentle waves caressing a pebbly beach." White spots in front of my eyes, a rushing sound in my ears, knees buckle, and boom! I'm out.

So, how was my mind going to react to a placenta? What would happen when I touched it? I took a deep breath and told myself that passing out in front of a bunch of Zanzibari midwives would be much less embarrassing than the circumcision waiting room.

I did not pass out while taking the specimen. I remembered to breathe through my mouth. Slowly. However, this became a minor victory as our training team progressed from Unguja, the main island of Zanzibar, to Pemba, the smaller and less populated island. Yes, fewer people meant fewer births, meant fewer placentas.

All of the midwives needed to practice creating a specimen at least once, and those having trouble needed to a few tries. We trained up to twenty midwives at a time. We needed placentas.

Placentas are no problem at Mnazi Mmoja, the main hospital in Unguja, where as many as forty women delivered in a twenty-four-hour period. We had called in advance and asked them to save a few to practice on. We arrived to find the placentas neatly lined up in metal kidney dishes. But Pemba Island posed a challenge. Of course, we had prepared all of the training materials that money could buy: surgical scissors, gloves, Whatman 960 filter paper, and pipettes galore. But what's a pipette with no placenta?

We planned to visit three health facilities in Pemba. Asma made phone calls to the first two facilities we would visit on the trip and gave me the thumbs up to indicate that we would have our placentas in Wete and Chake Chake Hospitals.

Then Asma reached out to the smallest facility, Michiweni Health Center, a small clinic that sometimes went days without deliveries. While Asma called, I attempted to alleviate my nervousness by fiddling with my computer. The midwife in charge of the maternity ward answered and I frowned at my keyboard while Asma inquired about her niece's graduation and whether mangos were ripe on her side of the island. But when the pleasantries ended, it turned out that the midwife was not at the health facility.

"Have her call the midwife on shift!" I yelled.

Asma was used to my meddling ways, and of course had already thought of that. She looked at me triumphantly as she put away her phone. There was a woman in labor at Micheweni; we would have our placenta.

The next day, we flew to Pemba. The plane angled down towards the small island, soft with rolling hills and lush green forests, sparkling turquoise waters lapping at rocky shorelines. I clutched the air sickness bag. Asma dabbed the sweat off of my forehead and spoke to me in a low, soothing tone. Veronica read her Kindle, apparently unaware that we were thousands of feet above the earth's surface in a tiny metal capsule. The flight from Unguja to Pemba takes around forty minutes, which is about nineteen minutes longer than my cool holds out on small planes.

We emerged from the airport to find our driver, Abdallah, waiting for us. We took off to Chake Chake Hospital, where there were plenty of placentas.

The trouble began at Wete, our second facility. We faced eighteen midwives and had only one placenta, despite Asma's call. The night shift midwife had not gotten the message and had sent two to the incinerator. We rationed our midwives—they only got one chance each. While I taught midwives how to obtain informed consent from women in labor, Asma paced the hallway talking on her cell phone. We had been told that we would have a placenta when we got to Micheweni, but now we knew to double-check. I raised my eyebrows at her as she walked into the room, and she sadly shook her head. The woman in labor had been referred to a larger facility because of complications. She was gone, with her placenta.

We conferred over lunch, fried chicken and chips, served in little aluminum trays. What would we do? We had traveled all this way, we had to train the midwives at the last facility, and we needed a placenta to train them. After a huddle, we decided we had no choice: we would take the sliced-up placenta from Wete to Micheweni. But how to transport it? I dumped my chips out of the aluminum container and held it out to Asma, who nodded once, then disappeared back into the labor ward.

Pemba's tropical heat was in full blast by the afternoon. We trudged back out to the car, hotter and sweatier than before. Asma carried a plastic bag with what looked like a spare packed lunch. She hesitated, then put the bag in the trunk with our other supplies.

When we reached Micheweni, handsome Abdallah gallantly opened the trunk and helpfully started to unload the supplies. Both Asma and I dove when he reached for the bag. I reached it first. "I'll take that one!"

The five midwives at Micheweni learned to create a study specimen on the driest, most sliced up placenta in the history of the island, which we were thankful to send to the facility's incinerator at the end of the day.

That night, I lay in bed enjoying the tropical warmth and humidity and lush night sounds outside my window and thought how much I loved my job. My day "in the office" had consisted of drama, critical thinking, willing myself not to pass out, and a bit of subterfuge—all set in a tropical paradise with a brilliant sidekick—and had ended in success.

*Cultural Interlude No. 2*

# Eye Contact Among Wazungu and Watanzania

**⚲⚲ Advice to Watanzania:** *Wazungu* put eye contact at the center of social interactions. Expect your *wazungu* friends and acquaintances to look you squarely in the eye the entire time you talk. Yes, it may be somewhat unsettling, but try your best. You are allowed to blink or to look away briefly, especially if it is clear that you are looking at something, like the rain that just started outside or a car alarm going off. Your *mzungu* friend will expect you to make sounds and/or nod your head occasionally *while maintaining eye contact.* He or she may feel unappreciated if you do not do this.

**⚲⚲ Advice to Wazungu:** Your *Watanzania* friends and acquaintances are sparing in their use of eye contact. It is considered challenging to stare someone in the eye while talking, so your polite friend might keep his gaze fixed at a spot nearby your head rather than looking in your eyes. Your *Mtanzania* friend might feel unappreciated if you do not laugh at least once in your conversation. Instead of connecting through eye contact, you can slap your friend's upturned hand when you appreciate what he is saying.

# 9

# A Statistician in Njombe

I had traveled to the green and rolling hills of the southern highlands, altitude of 4,925 feet above sea level. It was cold. I had forgotten to pack socks again. Living in the muggy heat of Dar es Salaam, I could never quite believe that it was going to be cold in Njombe. But it was, of course. I put on my one weird old sweater, which I had packed "just in case." If history was any precedent, I would end up wearing the ugly sweater every waking minute I was in Njombe, from the formal courtesy calls to regional officials to trips from my bed to the bathroom. However, fashion in Njombe was not high priority, where officials were used to Dar es Salaam counterparts shivering through meetings in borrowed coats.

I was going to see a male circumcision site with colleagues based in Njombe. The site had been set up in an unused market space in a village called Kifanya, about seventy kilometers south of Njombe. My colleague Saidi Mkungume and I were traveling together, though he and I were looking for different things: He was doing quality control of the surgery and I was looking at the documentation the surgeons kept, including adverse events, which was a marker for quality of service.

Male circumcision had been proven to prevent female-to-male transmission of HIV by up to 60 percent, and in Njombe, the region of Tanzania with the highest HIV prevalence, with roughly 15 percent of the adult population HIV positive, this was a much-needed intervention. Circumcision was offered free of charge, using experienced government health care providers. It also represented a cultural shift because circumcision was not traditional in the region. More and more, women preferred men who had been circumcised, and men responded to this preference by seeking the operation. Our work vehicle, a blue and yellow pickup truck, sported a painting of an attractive, conservatively dressed couple gazing meaningfully at each other, framed by the local euphemism for getting circumcised, *Dondosha Mkonosweta*. (Roll up your shirt sleeve.)

Our ride took almost three hours, two speeding down a narrow highway, and one bumping along a dirt road that had been a bit beaten up by the recent rainy season. In Kifanya, a town that had its share of tin-roofed houses amidst the thatch-roofed, mud-walled homes, we rolled to a stop in front of a large structure buzzing with activity.

Saidi, himself a surgeon, pointed out the town's government dispensary, a shabby-looking two-room building too small to fit the three hospital beds brought in to offer the service. Instead of using the tiny health facility, the medical team had converted an unused marketplace next door into a surgical center, complete with an area for group education, a tent for private HIV testing and counseling and physical exams, a surgical suite, and a post-operative resting area. A generator provided electricity for the autoclave and a tank provided running water. There was an open post-op area where the newly circumcised boys or men could sit and have a bottle of water and some biscuits before heading off on their walk home. Some came on foot from a distance of fifteen kilometers or more.

As reported to me by the team, the surgeons would show up in the morning to find a dozen or more boys waiting on the wooden benches. Men in their teens, who did not like to mix with the younger ones, would start dropping in in the afternoon. Occasionally a man in his thirties would pull one of the surgeons off to the side during a break and ask if he could come back for circumcision in the evening, when all of the younger clients had left.

After chatting with some of the clients and providers, I went in to the surgical theater to say hello to the surgeons. Most of them were women. For the first time ever, the Ministry of Health in Tanzania had allowed for task shifting of surgical duties to nurses. They were doing a great job. Some evaluations showed that nurses had a lower rate of adverse events than doctors.

The surgeons paused suturing or injecting anesthesia to look up and return my greeting. When I began my work as a program evaluator who kept track of trends in service delivery, such as number and age of clients and indicators of quality of care, they had humored me, but gradually they understood the importance of what I did and accepted me as part of the team. Someone dubbed me "the statistician," a name that stuck.

Saidi and I went to greet the health care provider who manned the tiny general health facility next door to the marketplace. Although she was not involved with the circumcision services, she had been briefed on what to do in case any men or boys experienced infections when the team had left Kifanya. She took a notebook from the table and drew columns into it, creating a guestbook for us to sign. When I asked her if she had ever had visitors from outside Tanzania visit her health facility, she laughed and shook her head. She gave us a tour, showing us the tiny room where she delivered up to twenty-five babies a month, with registers and medical supplies neatly stacked on the floor in the corner of the room. She told us that her main problem at the facility was a poor supply of electricity. She showed me a battery-operated light which she had designed herself. The contraption, which looked like a high school science project, had cost about $50 to create. I estimated that this might be roughly a quarter of her monthly salary. She had done it, she said, because she couldn't stand delivering another woman by the light of her cell phone.

I was proud to be part of the male circumcision team, knowing that in Njombe, for every fifteen men we circumcised, we averted one HIV infection. Saidi and I left the site, having collected the information we needed, knowing that on that night, like on the other thirteen they were camped in the area, the surgeons would work late offering circumcision to the boys and men in the Kifanya community.

# 10

# Blood Samples on Filter Paper

C lose your eyes and imagine you are walking into a hospital in Chake Chake on the island of Pemba. To get to the hospital, you drove through the narrow streets of the main market. The streets were congested with market stall displays of frilly girls' dresses, frying pans made from beaten tin, cans of Milo, long bars of soap to be wrapped in newspaper. The streets were so full of people that your car inched its way through. Cassava was being fried in cauldrons of bubbling oil. Men in white *kanzu* streamed into a mosque. Women wore black *bui-bui* that reach down to the ground. Children hurried to keep up with their mothers, passing by piles of food scraps, with scrawny kittens loping amongst. Flies buzzed around a heap of fish scraps near a food vendor.

You reach the hospital, which consists of a low buildings and covered walkways. The walls, once white, are now varying shades of gray, mottled with stains. The black-robed women who sit on the floor or walk the hallways wear colorful hijabs firmly tucked under their chins. The men wear round *kofia* hats. People bring flasks and baskets of food for relatives. There is chatter, bustle, but it is not the energetic hum of the market street. A child with eyelids darkened with kohl, maybe a year and a half old, toddles just outside of his mother's reach and crosses your path.

You walk down the tin-roofed walkway and turn left into the maternity ward. As you walk into the run-down structure, the air becomes closer around you. The floor, though swept clean, has so many scuff marks, stains, and cracks that there is no hope that it will ever gleam. There are two beds in the room off to your right, one with springs exposed and one with a mattress. At first glance, you think the awkwardly-placed beds are in the hallway for storage, but no, there is a woman lying in one. She is on her side with her back to you, wearing a long kaftan, and she is softly keening. A plastic basket sits by the bed. Inside there is a cloth, and probably the things she was told to bring with her because they are not in stock at the hospital: gloves, syringe, oxytocin, a plastic spread for the bed, a razor blade, two *kangas* to dry and wrap her newborn. Maybe some money to give to the nurses.

To your left, Bibi Rahima, the in-charge nurse of the maternity ward, sits on the edge of a table. The last time you saw her was during a training session on collecting placental blood samples a couple of months earlier. Your shared smile and her warm handshake reflect how much you enjoyed each other's company that day, how eager the nurses were to learn something new, the respect you felt for her when she picked up the task easily, and then coached others who were shy, or whose hands shook when trying to suction up drops of blood for the specimen.

The women from whom the specimens are collected have not had the preventative treatment for malaria, which they are supposed to get at least twice during their pregnancy. You are looking at the unprotected women to see if they are infected with the parasite.

A pregnant woman may have the malaria parasite and be unaware of it. Malaria in pregnancy can increase the risk of abortion, cause low birth weight for the baby and anemia for the mother. An anemic woman with a post-partum hemorrhage—one of the leading causes of maternal death in Tanzania—is much more likely to die.

The Zanzibar Ministry of Health, with support from international partners, has provided the preventative treatment during pregnancy as part of antenatal care. They have questions about the cost-effectiveness of continuing to provide malaria preventative treatment to pregnant women. Your study on malaria among pregnant women in Unguja and Pemba, the two islands of Zanzibar, will inform that decision.

As Bibi Rahima and you trade news on your lives since you last saw each other, two men come into the ward, carrying a young woman. Bibi Rahima sighs, puts down the register she was filling out, slides off the table, and finds her shoes. Two women follow close behind the men, holding a tiny *kanga*-wrapped bundle which can only be a baby. Bi Rahima leads them to the delivery room and shows them a bed onto which the men lower the woman. Another nurse hurries them out of the room. You are left standing alone as Rahima disappears into the delivery room.

The two accompanying women appear to shrink against the wall. They explain that the woman delivered at home but then had a lot of bleeding and could not breathe. They show you the fuzzy-headed baby wrapped in a green and white kanga, sleeping as completely as healthy newborns do.

To relieve the tension, you go to the nurses' station and find something to do. The forms that must be completed when a woman enters your study are in order: a client consent, a form which shows the gravidity of the woman, her hemoglobin level, the outcome of the birth, and the baby's birthweight.

You check supplies. While enough of the pipettes and filter paper are in evidence, all of the desiccant, which keeps the specimens dry, has turned pink in Pemba's overwhelming humidity. Order much more desiccant next time. The pen has been circled in tape with ASHA written on it in block letters. Taped onto the wall, slightly askew, is a hand-written sign detailing the steps in newborn resuscitation.

You walk back to the woman lying in the bed in the hallway. She is lying with her back to you. You gently touch her shoulder and ask her how she is doing. Her gaze is a bit unfocused as she regards you. You introduce yourself, and your accent in Swahili makes her smile despite her condition. She is twenty-three and this is her third child, you gather by glimpsing her card, which, in addition to her medical history, lists her husband's name and occupation. Her husband, Rashid Hashim, is a mechanic. You ask her where she is from and she says that she lives on the other side of the island, but is here in Chake Chake with her mother-in-law for the baby.

Her card states that she has not had sulfadoxine-pyrimethamine, the preventative drug for malaria, during her pregnancy, which means that she is eligible to be enrolled in your study. You ask a nurse you recognize from the training if she will take the consent of the client to be in the study. The nurse informs her about the study, that there are no risks and no direct benefits to being included in the study, and that if she agrees to be in the study, a few drops of blood will be taken from the placenta before it is discarded. The nurse waits as the woman squeezes her eyes shut for a contraction. The woman somewhat breathlessly asks if it will hurt, and the nurse assures her that this will be done after the placenta is removed from her body and that there is no pain involved. The woman agrees to be in the study, and the nurse signs the consent form on her behalf. You know that from here, after the birth, after the woman has been tended to, this nurse will put the woman's placenta in a surgical pan, find the maternal side, locate a site in the placenta away from the cord, and make a deep incision with a scissor. The nurse will then take a pipette, suck up blood, and squeeze out five drops onto little round spots on the filter paper. The filter paper will be put in a rack to dry. This is your specimen.

Bi Rahima is now washing her hands under a bucket with a tap, which they have used in the maternity ward since last April, when the piped water stopped flowing. Inquiries in the matter were not clear as to whether the lack of running water was due to the hospital not paying its bill to the water vendor for over a year or the rusted piping that finally broke beyond repair. As you catch her eye, she sighs and says, "220 over 120," referring to the woman's blood pressure.

"Do you have magnesium sulfate?" you ask, saying a little prayer that she does.

"Yes, I gave her."

You exhale a sigh of relief internally, not showing Bi Rahima. At least the convulsions will likely be prevented. Bi Rahima explains that the woman also had a retained placenta that they manually removed.

Bi Rahima is exasperated. Apparently, the woman had been to a nearby health facility twice complaining of difficulty breathing, but no one had checked her blood pressure to look for preeclampsia. Even upon admission to the maternity ward, her blood pressure hadn't been checked. It's true, she admits, the blood pressure cuff in the maternity ward is broken, but there is one in the antenatal care clinic. Why hadn't the nurses gone to get it?

You recall a conversation from yesterday with your good friend, a doctor at Zanzibar's busiest maternity ward, where easily thirty women a day give birth. Why aren't systems working? Why are women still dying of hypertensive disease in health facilities when the medicine is known, not overly expensive, and all nurses have been trained on how to detect and treat it? You remember your friend's grimace. So many factors, she said. First, the drugs are not there half the time. They have either been stolen, used up, or delayed in transit. Sometimes they arrive already expired. If the drugs are there, critical equipment that could help in the diagnosis, such as blood pressure cuffs, are missing or broken. Some health facility staff are corrupt, demanding payment for supplies that the hospital has in stock and that are supposed to be provided for free. And, she adds, you have to understand. Nurses are burned out. They work almost every day of the week, delivering seemingly endless babies, in hospitals that are so overcrowded that there are sometimes two women per bed, sometimes women are camped out on the floor. Sometimes women give birth in the pre-natal ward a foot away from their neighbor, with no privacy. The nurses are paid less than $300 a month, not enough to feed their families or send their kids to decent schools. They see babies and women die because supplies are missing. They see that the hospital management doesn't care enough to make sure the drugs are there, and eventually they don't care anymore either.

A bed has been wheeled in to take the woman from the delivery room to the female ward, where she will be kept for two days to make sure her blood pressure is controlled. The lab will check her hemoglobin level. Bi Rahima sighs again. She might need blood. The blood pressure can mask shock, and with the retained placenta the woman has possibly lost a great deal of blood. From her resigned expression, you don't want to ask about the availability of blood in the hospital. You know Rahima well enough to be sure that she will come in on her off day to make sure that the woman gets what she needs to survive.

You collect your filter paper samples now, checking that every sample has a client card, a consent form, and the filing papers. You pack everything into plastic bags. As you leave, you see Bi Rahima sink wearily, but carefully, into the rickety chair in the nursing station. Another nurse enters the nursing station and behind you, you hear them laughing, a good proper "hey hey!" of amusement, and you realize that, in Pemba, life goes on, and with it, a good laugh.

Later that day you will strap yourself into a seat on a small plane with your 203 filter paper specimens in a box on your lap, headed for Unguja, taking with you 202 women's birth stories. All live births, according to the forms. That means 202 women with 203 babies (one set of twins), a trace of whose placentas (forgotten on the joy of hearing their babies' first cries) were captured on filter paper. A tiny piece of their story becomes part of your story. In the airplane with the box on your lap, you say a prayer that all of those babies and mothers lead long, happy, and healthy lives.

*Cultural Interlude No. 3*

# Taboos in American and Tanzanian Society

**⚤ Advice to Wazungu:** Ladies, get out your washing powder. It is considered extremely rude in Tanzanian culture to make someone else wash your underwear. It is the height of rudeness to make a man wash your underwear. A man washing his wife's underwear is actually a famed example of a defeated man. Tanzanian ladies wash their own underwear in the shower each evening and hang their *chupi* to dry discreetly in the bathroom.

*Wazungu* friends, do not hand anything to your Tanzanian friend with your left hand, most especially food items.

**⚤ Advice to Watanzania:** It is considered shockingly rude in America to pick your nose in public. Plugging up one nostril with your finger and blowing the snot at the ground is also impolite. Belching at any time, even after a well-appreciated meal, is not good etiquette and should always be followed up with a heartfelt, "Excuse me!" If you inadvertently burp, you may wish to act surprised and say, "Where did that come from?"

Please avoid staring at strangers in public. It is considered rude.

Both cultures find farting rude, but it is more embarrassing in Tanzanian culture.

##### ::::: 11 :::::

# Summer Reading

On a summer visit to my parents in the States, I spotted a new book, *The Lacuna* by Barbara Kingsolver, in sturdy hardcover in an exciting shade of yellow on my parents' bookshelf. I couldn't wait to get my hands on it.

Except I never did. The summer passed. I read a John Irving book instead. I was too busy running around after the kids. I meant to pack *The Lacuna* to take back to Tanzania, but forgot to, so I would have to wait another year to read my only unread Barbara Kingsolver book.

Fast forward a year. We were home for summer holidays again. I headed upstairs to the bookshelf to claim my prize, *The Lacuna*, with its cheery yellow jacket. It wasn't there! Aha, it turned out that my brother had borrowed it. No worries, I was going up to Jer and Audrey's in a couple of weeks, I would get it there.

Books are well-loved in my brother's household, which is not to say they have an easy life there. They are stacked so thickly on the coffee table, we actually have no idea what the coffee table looks like, or in fact, if it is a table at all. Books in my brother's house might host a glass of water or orange juice, and it might spill. Books may be nosed by the dog, used as flying objects by my nephews, subjected to farm dirt drifting into their pages, or have a sofa cushion inserted as a bookmark.

I found *The Lacuna* living in the study bookshelf, a book's most privileged spot in the household. And then.... How did the summer fly by so quickly? I still hadn't read the book, but this time I took it with me. Finally, back in Dar es Salaam, I began to read. It was not love at first page. I found it so different from Kingsolver's other books, I had a hard time getting into it, until page 102. Then I was hooked.

I took the boys to swim in our compound's pool and slipped the book into my bag. Tadzio had just finished his first week of kindergarten and Janusz of fifth grade. It was a Friday afternoon and they were fighting about water guns, who splashed whom, who made a face at whom, and who stepped on whose fingers. I took out *The Lacuna*, pretending the pandemonium was not happening. Not so lucky. Tadzio collapsed in a full on, toddler-style tantrum, letting out all the emotional steam of the week. I grabbed towels, goggles, shoes, water guns, and inflatable toys as best I could and carried my blubbering child home fireman style, tears and snot running down his face.

I didn't have a chance to return to my book for several days. When I finally got ready for a couple of good hours on the sofa with *The Lacuna*, it was nowhere to be found. I stomped around the house several times looking for it, before I realized I must have left it at the pool. More busy days passed, in which I meant to get to the pool but didn't. By the time I did, it was a whole week later. I snooped around, looking under the chairs, but no cheery yellow hardcover book greeted me. The pool guy told me to check with the guards to see if it had been left with them. I found this very unlikely, but dutifully tried. Nope, no book.

I was bereft. After waiting a year and a half, was this my fate with *The Lacuna*?

Life in Dar es Salaam could be stressful in many ways. There was the heat, the dust, the traffic, the kids. There was crime to worry about. There was the gardener's wife who needed an operation. There was the crumbling health system that we worked at like ants to try to improve, only to hear increasingly discouraging stories of the delays, corruption, and people dying in corridors. As my father-in-law used to say, in the government health sector, the health care providers pretended to work and the government pretended to pay them. There were robberies and potholes and petrol mixed with kerosene that would knock your car's engine.

To counteract this stress, my friend Ranahnah and I often went to the Oriental Spa. The spa was tucked down a very dusty, very bumpy road in Msasani. The road, muddy in the rainy season and dusty in the dry season, was a taste of Swahili life, with people strolling by hand-in-hand, kids in all shades of brown hanging out in doorways or playing in the street, a born-again Christian church buzzing with shouts and songs, a guy on a bicycle melodically chanting the names of the greens he was selling. Interspersed with shops selling *kangas* and vegetables, two new apartment buildings rose up awkwardly, building materials so shoddy the buildings started falling apart before they were finished. The road was so bad that you had to roll through slowly, which allowed for the smell of frying cassava to waft in through the car windows.

The spa, a curious oasis amidst the Swahili bustle of the street, was situated in a repurposed house. Inside, the sounds of the street muted, you found flower arrangements, white stones, cushions, and hand-rolled towels. You could have an hour-and-a-half massage, complete with a petite lady walking on your back, for a very affordable price. You could sit at a plastic table on the porch and get a beer, a bowl of pho or some spring rolls, or strong iced coffee with sweetened condensed milk. Although there was a menu, it always felt more like you had walked into a family house and they shared the contents of the kitchen with you.

The only downside was the music, always the same plinky elevator music of undetermined bent, perhaps Vietnamese folk songs. Ranahnah and I always meant to bring our own CDs, but we always forgot.

A few months after the book went missing, I went to Oriental Spa for my de-stress. As I sipped my juice, my eye wandered to the bookshelf. A gasp, then a little chuckle sneaked out of me when I saw the cheery yellow spine of *The Lacuna* amidst the Oriental Spa books.

As the Vietnamese lady walked on my back, I made up a story of the book's journey from our compound's pool in Masaki to the bookshelf in the Oriental Spa. I imagined the relief of the underpaid guard, as he sold the book to the man who passes by our compound selling shoes, allowing the guard to get on a *dala-dala* instead of walking two hours to get home. The shoe guy doesn't do business in books, but his cousin used to work as a driver for a Vietnamese guy who went to Oriental Spa every night to hang out. The cousin doesn't work for the Vietnamese guy anymore, but during the nights at Oriental Spa waiting for his passenger to get drunk enough to take home, he started a relationship with the thin shy young lady who chops vegetables for the kitchen. He still goes by to see her occasionally, though he knows he shouldn't, and his wife suspects his infidelity. The young lady doesn't want to see him anymore and told the guard at Oriental Spa not to let the driver in. The last time the driver went he brought the book as a peace offering to the guard to let him in so he could try to talk to the lady once more. He told the guard to sell the book to the Vietnamese owners. When the guard presented the book to the owners, they offered him an insultingly low amount for it, but he took it because his elderly sister told him that if he didn't come home with dried fish today he shouldn't come home at all.

There are no limits to the stories, the routes, and the hands the book could have passed through to be sitting there on the shelf in front of me. They would all remain unknown to me, especially since the ladies at Oriental Spa spoke neither English nor Kiswahili. At that moment, all I knew was, I was reunited with my book. I slipped it into my backpack.

I read it and on another visit, put it back onto the spa's bookshelf so it could continue its journey down Dar es Salaam's slipstream of serendipity and survival.

*Cultural Interlude No. 4*

# Being Direct and Disposition

ͼͼ **Advice to Wazungu:** Your Tanzanian friend will generally state his opinions in a roundabout way rather than directly, especially if there is any displeasure. Look out for the understated negative. When things are described as "a little bit good" (*nzuri kidogo*), they may actually be very, very bad.

Please understand that it is very difficult for your Tanzanian friend to say "no" in response to a question. Rephrase the question so that the answer can be "yes." For example, "Did you get the new tire for the car?" (Answer: No, I did not get a new tire for the car.) This can be rephrased as, "Did you get the new tire for the car, or were they all out of tires at the shop?" (Answer: Yes, I did not get a new tire for the car since they were all out of tires at the shop.)

ͼͼ **Advice to Watanzania:** Your *mzungu* friend may say things that are so negative that you get worried. For example, or he or she may say things like "it was a disaster" or "it was a nightmare" in relation to puzzlingly minor incidents, like a phone call with a poor connection or the food taking long to arrive for lunch. Your *mzungu* friend may have days where she seems sad, gets angry easily, or doesn't want to talk. This is a condition that *wazungu* refer to as "having a bad hair day" or "being grumpy." She is not sick and does not require medicine or need to go lay down. This is similar to the *Mtanzania* condition of having a lot of thoughts (*mawazo mengi*). While this is normal for *wazungu,* if she lives in Tanzania long enough, she will stop having this condition.

# 12

# Gilly Arthur

I posthumously bestow the following award on my friend, Gilly Arthur:

## Best Mad Scientist Award

When I visited Gilly's office, I stood in the doorway and leaned to one side or another so that I could see her around the precariously stacked piles of papers littering her desk. Gilly always gave me the same greeting: "Oh, hello," as if surprised to see me, even if I had told her I was coming. She stepped over text books or manuals sitting on the floor to come around from behind the desk and give me a hug. Her mind was as full as her office. At any time, she had at least eight projects on the burner: protocols, papers, writing workshops, or review processes. She had the sharpest mind for science of anyone I've ever met. In true Mad Scientist form, Gilly didn't give a hoot about wearing dressy clothes. Gilly had a loose relationship with fundamentals of organization. She was extremely outspoken and would not back down from a point when she knew she was right. Our friend, Peter McElroy, tells me he could always count on Gilly telling him when an idea was "utter rubbish."

Gilly took care of people. All people. Although her job title was Associate Director of Science at Centers for Disease Control (CDC) Tanzania, Gilly was known unofficially as the CDC doctor. The one you went to for advice, the one who always had time to listen to you, the one who fixed you with an intent go-on-I'm-listening look as soon as you started talking. Her gardener received medical care; her kids' nanny received life counseling; HIV-infected clients at Mwananyamala Hospital received the kindest care of their lives. Even her daughter Joni's chicken received great care. A coop with a ramp was built and Gilly took notes during a specialized consult on poultry-rearing with my mother-in-law. You mentioned an illness to Gilly at your own risk, since she would prescribe a treatment and stubbornly stand beside you until you complied with her orders. If you had a fever and didn't want to be tested and treated, you'd best not mention it to Gilly, who would cheerfully march you to the nearest laboratory and order the diagnostics for you. And wait in the lobby until you got them.

I speak Swahili very well, which only makes sense. I married into the country and spent much of my adult life there. Gilly learning Swahili was more remarkable—I think she did it for a combination of wanting to help people and not missing out on any of the fun.

Mind you, she did have a heavy British accent when speaking Swahili.

Gilly's adventurousness, spontaneity, intelligence, and caring hit a perfect ten with me. Her friendship reached me in a place that was made only for her. As soon as we met, we were friends. It wasn't really a discuss-each-other's-problems type of friendship. We certainly did, and her support was considered, empathetic, and pragmatic when I asked for it. Rather, the heart of our friendship was creative adventure-seeking, both within our profession and in life.

Late one Thursday night, Gilly called me and said, as if surprised that it was me on the other end of the line, "Oh, hello! There's a Hindu festival on in town, do you want to go see it?"

Um, sure, I guess.

"Right, I'll just swing round and pick you up."

I grabbed my sandals, sprayed on some mosquito repellent, and heard the sound of Gilly's car idling outside. I asked her what the festival was. She didn't know. I asked her where. She didn't know that either, but why not just cruise around the Indian section of Dar es Salaam and see if we found something? We drove around narrow streets in Upanga until we came across a well-lit temple, decorated with flowers, with people going in and out. Gilly jumped out of the car, started up a discussion with an Indian gentleman going into the temple, and he invited us in.

Another time, we attended the wedding of a mutual friend, a young American Muslim woman marrying a Tanzanian man, also from a Muslim family. The wedding was held in a hall in an old building in downtown Dar es Salaam. Gilly arranged for a taxi to drop us downtown so that we didn't have to worry about parking cars. This was good judgment. We arrived about an hour and a half later than the invitation time. This was good judgment too. As we were about to head up the stairs to the wedding, I turned around to say something to Gilly and noticed that she had put something on her head. I looked more closely.

"Gilly," I said, "is that a skirt on your head?"

"Oh, yeah," she said, "I thought it better to, you know, cover my head, but I didn't have that proper scarf thingy, so I just grabbed this. Does it look alright?" Bad judgment.

"No, it does not look alright!" I said. "Take that skirt off your head immediately!"

Gilly sheepishly removed the skirt, saying, "I just thought... you know."

Gilly and I watched a dance performance at the National Museum, trying to be open-minded about a Swedish/Tanzanian modern dance collaboration. At the break, an announcer mentioned that a car outside had been broken into and read out the plate number. It was Gilly's car, and we rushed outside to find that the back window had been broken. Nothing important seemed to be missing from the car. Gilly cheerfully brushed away the glass and we decided to leave the modern dance to people with more sophisticated tastes than ours. We headed off to have a drive along the moonlit ocean instead. The breeze coming in the broken window was delightful.

When Gilly told me she was moving to London in a month's time, it felt like another one of her crazy adventure stories. "Well, I guess we'll make Joni's birthday party a leaving do as well," she told me, as she thrust upon me an enormous plastic bag full of the most careworn clothes I had ever seen, to be distributed to children in need.

Gilly's departure from Dar was the first time I had experienced the phenomenon that haunts the expat world: when a good friend leaves, when someone you feel so close to or rely on for some part of your life is suddenly half a world away. Friendships are deeper for the risk of departure, but it is a hard and sad adjustment when your dear friend leaves. It had never happened to me before.

One night in February 2013, my phone rang. I was in our house in Dar es Salaam. It was a quiet night for me, in a time when my evenings and nights were lonely and I spent my time writing or working late. I could see it was a call from the UK, from the 41 area code, and was delighted to hear Gilly's voice over the line. But I could tell immediately that things were not alright. She managed to say, "We've had some terrible news."

But then her voice broke up, became whispery and strangled on the other end of the line. My mind raced to imagine the bad news before she could tell me. I imagined that one of our mutual friends in Tanzania had died. All my years in Africa led me to believe that the bad news generally occurred in Tanzania rather than in England. As she choked out the news between sobs, my insides turned to ice as I realized she was speaking about herself.

Gilly. Gilly was telling me that she what? Had been diagnosed with…did she say… terminal illness? A brain tumor? She was crying so hard she could barely speak. I was somewhere between not understanding her, not believing what she was telling me, and not wanting to make her say it again. When she hung up, I went outside into the garden, where the night was velvety warm and the trees were silhouetted against the moonlight and I cried and cried.

Gilly insisted that she did not want sympathy, she wanted news. I filled my evenings with writing emails to cheer her up, with news from Dar es Salaam. I sent off email after email. Her responses got shorter, full of spelling errors, and then less frequent, as she started to lose vision.

At some point, responses stopped coming, but I continued. Writing Gilly became a ritual I used to pacify my sadness, shots in the dark, not knowing if I was saying the right thing, the wrong thing, or if she was able to read the emails at all. Early on I felt like I was writing for her, and as time went on and I didn't know if she was getting the emails, I knew I was writing for myself.

I have close to a hundred emails to Gilly in my sent mail file from March 2013. Early on, they are full of advice. I was trying to come up with solutions, looking for little intellectual victories over the cancer.

*I was thinking about how you and I both have been the ones in charge of so much: always expecting ourselves to be competent, on top of everything (albeit usually late and, yes, quite messy). I was thinking that, if this diagnosis had happened to me, I would be trying to stay on top of everything in the household in addition to the treatment and all the emotions/hopes/ fears. If this is happening to you, I hope you can give yourself a break with the household.*

Another time:

*Hope the treatment goes well, and if it doesn't, remember that today might not represent all the other days to come.*

As the weeks progressed, the emails turned into ongoing logs of life in Dar, or anywhere else I went. All Gilly wanted was news, and her way of coping with illness, loss of vision, seizures, chemotherapy, and hair loss was beyond the scope of my advice. My emails were labeled "Hello from Dar" or "Hello from Mwanza," and they were full of cheer that I didn't feel. I'll write whatever you want, Gilly, to make you smile.

*News of Dar today: RAIN! Just as I roused sleepy boys, the pattering started and I thought of diving back into bed and canceling everything, until I remembered that I was the grown up. So we dashed off in the rain and made it to school damp but on time.*

And another day:

*I tried to look for the trees you planted, but to be honest the light was in my eyes and I was trying to avoid getting hit by oncoming traffic and avoid pedestrians and I couldn't figure out which were the trees you planted. As you know, bicycling in Dar is not actually a good activity to combine with looking for something smaller than a house. If you remember where they are, roughly, let me know so I can give you an update.*

I visited Gilly twice in London. The first time, I walked up Carver Lane, a pretty London street flush with roses, not knowing what to expect, telling myself that I wouldn't cry no matter how she was. And then she opened the door and she was just my friend Gilly. I was amazed by her intrepid spirit. A loss of sight in her left eye and seizures that she called "the wobbles" hadn't slowed her down. We walked the kids to school in the morning, with Joni zipping ahead on a scooter, with the dog on the leash, chatting about parenting. Since she had misplaced her wig, she opted for a hat instead.

The day I arrived she had to take her chemotherapy. She had me help identify the correct medication, since she couldn't read the labels, but wouldn't let me handle the pills. Before taking them, she rolled them in her hand like a pair of lucky dice, saying, "Come on, chemo, do your thing!"

My gladness in finding Gilly so herself and with such an indomitable spirit was interspersed with moments of chilling sadness that cut me to the bone. Overhearing Gilly talking to a health insurance agent over the phone, every time she mentioned that her illness was terminal, her voice would go down to a stage whisper, to prevent the kids from hearing it.

On the second day of my visit, Gilly announced that we were

going to go to an art museum and for a walk in the park. The museum was a small but lovely one, and we wandered peacefully through, sometimes taking in the paintings together and sometimes individually. The park was nearby, beautiful, green, encircling a lake with swans gliding.

We paused and sat at a table. Gilly faced me. This was the moment I came here for and the moment I feared. Her voice started out clear but grew shaky as she told me how afraid she was to leave her children. I put my arm around her, and I could feel it, like metal conducting cold, her horror and despair at leaving Stan and Joni behind. It was the closest I have ever been to pure human anguish, and it was my friend's. Just seeing her anguish hurt me, and yet she was living it. It seemed like a bottomless well into which one could scream endlessly. I talked about how Steve would do wonderfully, how her sisters would be there with motherly love for the kids. Somehow, with my arms around her, I told her, without crying, that her children would be alright when she died.

The words I spoke to Gilly were, to me, a sheen of rainbow-colored oil resting on the surface of water: tawdry, illusory, incapable of supporting anything. I hated my helplessness to provide her with something real. I floundered with hollow words that I didn't believe. I felt like I was supposed to be throwing a life preserver to my friend and instead threw a twig, and then we both acted as if I had helped.

I didn't believe it. I didn't believe that the kids would be alright. Gilly and I had worked hard, analyzed and re-analyzed our parenting because it was our mission, our job, the work that really mattered above all else. We also both believed that without us there to be the mother, that all of the work, our most amazing creations and most fundamental responsibility, would fall to the ground and shatter.

In March, when I was in Baltimore for a meeting, there was a renegade snowstorm. The emails from London hadn't come from Gilly for months. Instead they were updates from Gilly's sister, Hazel, or friend, Posy, and they were full of updates of a medical nature supplemented by a brief anecdote about Gilly. This time, the email was grim: Gilly was in the hospital. It sounded like she may not come home. I changed my flight to go to London.

It was snowing outside and I was alone in a hotel room that looked out over the grayest, coldest urban landscape I could imagine. For some reason the lack of even the tiniest hint of color seemed horrifying, and then it all swam in a blur of tears as I realized Gilly was going to die.

This time the email I wrote seemed to come from somewhere on its own. I knew that she would not get it, and even if she did, she would not be well enough to understand it. It was to be as unseen and pointless and important as wishing on a star.

> *My dearest Gilly,*
>
> *I am in a snowstorm in Baltimore. The air is cloudy with snow, nothing is clear. Although I can see the beauty in it, I know how cold it is out there.*
>
> *I want it to be clear.*
>
> *You are in a snowstorm in London. It's cloudy, you can't see the horizon. It's not what you have been living for years.*
>
> *I want it to be clear for you.*
>
> *I want the sun to come back out and shine on you.*
>
> *I want it so much that it is my truth today. Today, the sun will shine on you, Gilly. Today, I will walk through a doorway and not be in a snowstorm in Baltimore but will see you walking up the beach in a wetsuit in the warm sun, sand clinging to your hair, and I will be in awe of my funny, smart, and*

*amazing friend who can ride the wind across the ocean. I'm going to hear the rumble of a car, look out of the window, and laugh to see you pulling up outside my door with a book in your hand and an adventure on your mind, ready to take me somewhere I haven't been before. In my endless meetings today, I am going to look up from a table full of people who haven't bothered, and you will be there, telling us something really new and insightful, making me proud to be your friend.*

*Today, I promise the sun is going to shine on you, Gilly.*

*I am holding you up in the sun's light with my love. All of the people who love you are holding you up and you know how determined we can be. You are held by an unbreakable web of love, of people who know you inside and out, flaws and strengths, and think you are one of the greatest people we will ever have the good fortune to meet. I am powering the sunshine to you today from the snowstorm in Baltimore. I know it will find you, and join with the warmth of all of the other people who love you.*

*Love from Marya*

My friend Sara insisted I would know what to do when I got there, but leaving the tube station to walk up the street to the hospital, I wasn't so sure. What would I say? What if I cried? But once perched on her hospital bed, I had the pleasure of helping with mundane tasks, unprofoundly drinking tea in a Styrofoam cup, and making her laugh with an abbreviated version of my trolley run through Shoppers Plaza supermarket in Dar. When it was time to leave, and I knew I was seeing her for the last time, I was able to whisper in my friend's ear what I needed to tell her, that I loved her, that she had enriched my life. I kissed her cheek. I didn't cry. I told her that her kids would be alright. And this time, I believed it.

Because a thought had been growing in my head for months. Maybe those words I said to Gilly in the London park, though they were hollow and meaningless to me at the time, were actually true. Maybe the mothering and parenting, the love and work, our life's most important creation, do continue without us. The work that Gilly did, and which I do, was to create a family, yet it is not a breakable creation that we hold together, a fragile ball that our absence will cause to fall and shatter. Rather, all of our work is in growing strong saplings that will continue to grow without us. The kids will be alright.

Five months later, I came again to London for Gilly's memorial service. I had the joy of meeting so many of her friends and family. We shared story after story of Gilly's amazing, adventurous spirit. I started to have a glimpse of what lay around the corner, beyond the ragged feeling of grief, to what I would miss. I listened to an audio recording of Gilly and me in the back garden on Carver Road, with Gilly recounting stories of the kids and of soapy cereal and spoiled milk in Dar es Salaam, with both of us laughing, and remembered what had gotten lost in the painful vortex of her illness: the chemistry of our friendship, the places where she fit so well in my life, her humor, her intelligence, her passion for life, our connection.

I wonder why we have to grieve, why we can't delight in the enrichment that a person brings to our life, but rather have to grapple with the pain of them not being there anymore. I do believe that as time goes by this shifts. It has for me with Gilly. The happiness for having had the opportunity to know her is catching up with the grief of losing her.

# 13

# Dr. Kumpuni

No matter where I was in Tanzania, if I mentioned that I was Dr. Kumpuni's daughter-in-law, doctors would smile. "Dr. Kumpuni? Really? How is he?" And then would come a story of Dr. Kumpuni's best snappy line in an emergency situation, or how he stepped aside to let a student take over a delivery, only stepping in when the student was clearly over his or her head. It didn't matter where I was: I heard similar stories in a mission hospital in Kagera, a regional hospital in Morogoro, or a health center in Iringa. He had either taught or was a colleague to most doctors in Tanzania.

My father-in-law, the late Dr. Hamadi Kitindi Kumpuni, was born in the Tabora region of Tanzania in 1943. His father, a respected man related to the famous Chief Fundikira, worked for Tabora Dairies, a British farming enterprise, and later for the British colonial administration. Kitindi, as my father-in-law was called, was one of two boys born to his mother, Binti Mohamedi, who was his father's second wife. Binti Mohamedi did not like being a second wife and left the boys with her husband's family for many years.

Kitindi's childhood was not easy. He and his older brother were not treated well by their stepmother in their mother's absence. They

*The whole family
(Dr. Kumpuni,
Bogusia, Medzio,
and baby Marian)
in Dodoma,
in 1974.*

fended for themselves, many nights cooking *ugali* on a fire they built after walking home from school and finishing their chores. The walk to their primary school, which they did by themselves, was over five kilometers.

Kitindi did well in primary school, and his marks earned him a place in the prestigious Tabora Boys Secondary School, a boarding school in Tabora town. Tanzania's first president, Julius Nyerere, also schooled at Tabora Boys. Kitindi graduated in 1961. At this time, he spoke Nyamwezi, the tribal language in Tabora; Swahili, the national language; and English, used for secondary school.

Waiting for his marks and to see what he could do next, Kitindi went to Dar es Salaam to stay with an uncle, Simon Nghwaya, who is always referred to in the family as Mzee Simon (Elder Simon).

Mzee Simon was an author and a journalist with the government newspaper. Kitindi got a job as an office assistant for the newspaper.

In the newspaper, Kitindi read an announcement about scholarships to study medicine in either Bulgaria or Poland. Kitindi applied to go to Poland, since he had had a pen pal from there when he studied at Tabora Boys.

Kitindi was nineteen years old when he arrived in Poland in 1963. Like other foreign students, he spent a year learning Polish before he could start his medical studies. He was tall, slim, handsome, and funny. During his first year of medical school in the town of Lodz, he was introduced to the beautiful younger cousin of a friend from medical school. Her name was Boguslawa (Bogusia) Halina Kawczynska, my mother-in-law. They were married in 1966 and four years later, my former husband, Medzio Medi Pawel Kumpuni, was born. Medzio was one of the few black kids in Lodz. Kitindi (now Dr. Kumpuni) finished his medical studies in 1973, and moved to Tanzania with his wife and son. This was a brave move for Bogusia and Medzio, who spoke no Swahili and had never been outside of Poland before. When Bogusia moved to Tanzania, she found a small community of other families in which the husbands had studied in Eastern Europe and brought back wives. There were women from Bulgaria, Czechoslovakia, Hungary, Russia, and Poland adjusting to and raising families in Tanzania. The family settled first in the remote Newala district of Mtwara, where Dr. Kumpuni was the district medical officer.

In 1974, shortly after moving the family to Dodoma, Dr. Kumpuni received a letter from the minister of health, informing him that he was to go to Cuba to specialize in obstetrics and gynecology. President Nyerere had been to Cuba, and Fidel Castro had told him to send over ten doctors for specialization. Dr. Kumpuni went to the minister's office to let him know that he could not go, since his wife, who was from another country and had only recently relocated to Tanzania, was expecting a baby in a few months. The minister told him flatly that if he did not go to Cuba, he would never practice medicine in Tanzania. Within a few weeks, Dr. Kumpuni was in Havana, learning Spanish so that he could complete his specialization. Medzio's younger brother, Marion, was born in Dodoma in 1974, delivered by a friend and colleague who had been entrusted to take care of Bogusia in Dr. Kumpuni's absence.

Dr. Kumpuni managed to get enough time off from his studies to move the family back to Poland while he completed the three years of specialization. He now spoke Nyamwezi, Swahili, English, Polish, and Spanish fluently.

In 1978, the family moved back to Tanzania, and Dr. Kumpuni started working at Bugando Hospital in Mwanza as the head of obstetrics and gynecology. Medzio and Marion grew up going to Nyakahoja Holy Family Catholic School. Dr. Kilala, a friend and colleague, had married Herta, a German lady, and the four mixed race boys, Medzio, Marion, Chris, and Deryck, were inseparable.

In 1986, Dr. Kumpuni was asked to work in the Ministry of Health. He and the family moved to Dar es Salaam, with the exception of Medzio who stayed behind in Mwanza to finish secondary school. Dr. Kumpuni worked at the Ministry of Health for five years, but missed clinical practice. In 1991 he resigned from the ministry and started working at Muhimbili Hospital, the country's largest medical facility.

Dr. Kumpuni was one of the hospital's most hardworking doctors. He taught medical students, he delivered babies, he performed surgery, at all hours of the night. His passion for work stayed with him throughout his life. He was never not a doctor, even when at leisure over the weekend in his home, when neighbors, friends, and relatives would show up with their pregnant wives to have a quiet conversation on the porch. He had numerous opportunities to work in private practices. Though he sometimes consulted for prestigious hospitals in Dar es Salaam, he continued to work in the government hospital, delivering babies for Tanzania's poorest women and being paid a very nominal government salary.

Bogusia, who quickly became fluent in Swahili, started working as an administrator for Christian Social Services Commission in Mwanza. She continued her work for the organization in Dar es Salaam and was an integral part of CSSC's work for over twenty years.

Dr. Kumpuni worked for Muhimbili, both practicing obstetrics and teaching medical students, until 2005. Then, at the age of sixty-five, instead of retiring, Dr. Kumpuni started teaching at Hubert Kairuki Medical School. The founder of the school, Dr. Hubert Kairuki, was a classmate of Dr. Kumpuni's from Tabora Boys School.

There was no question that Dr. Kumpuni would work his whole life. The practice of obstetrics and gynecology was as integral to him as his dedication to his family, and so was the volunteer work he did for organizations such as the National Muslim Foundation of Tanzania, BAKWATA. When he passed away in 2014, the dining room table was piled with stacks of papers he was grading.

Dr. Kumpuni was famous for his humor, for never getting ruffled or angry, and for not considering himself above anyone else. He was a favorite for joking with and teasing everyone, but he was deeply respected for his unwavering dedication to helping people who didn't have money or access to expensive health care. Almost all of his colleagues, the original stars of medicine in Tanzania who had specialized abroad, went into private practice. But not Dr. Kumpuni. He embodied the ideals of Julius Nyerere, Tanzania's beloved first president: dedication to service to fellow Tanzanians, equality of all Tanzanians, and concern for people rather than making money. For that, he was deeply respected.

Dr. Kumpuni prided himself on being a simple man. Even after Tanzania's austere years of socialism ended, he didn't acquire expensive material things. When he moved from Mwanza to Dar es Salaam, Dr. Kumpuni kept the same car he had driven for years: a Volkswagen Beetle. He crossed the Serengeti Plains with that Beetle, and kept driving it for the next 15 years in Dar es Salaam. On more than one occasion, a newly hired guard at Muhimbili would shout at Dr. Kumpuni to move the battered car out of the doctor's parking lot. When off duty, Dr. Kumpuni could be found at his house, in shorts, with no shirt, with a hose, watering his banana plants and papaya trees.

To me, Dr. Kumpuni was Baba. I knew well of his fame. And yet, I knew him primarily as a father and as the patriarch of the Kumpuni family.

Every time Medzio and I moved into a new house, Baba would come and inspect it. He and Mama would stay long enough to have a cup of tea, and then head home. Every Sunday, when Mama prepared a feast for lunch, we would sit around and exchange stories. Baba was unflappable, opinionated, and always in good humor, with a bit of a twinkle in his eye. He laughed, teased, and told stories. He called me his daughter, not his daughter-in-law.

When Baba was diagnosed with cancer, which had already metastasized, he did not tell us for a couple of weeks. He knew very well what his prognosis was. Despite the tremendous amount of pain he must have endured, he was stoic. Only once did Medzio find him leaning against the kitchen counter in pain; all other times, he hid it.

When Baba passed away, just three months after the diagnosis of cancer, the outpouring of condolences was massive. The medical community, the universities, the friends, the family, and dozens of people we didn't even know came to pay respects.

My father-in-law, Dr. Kumpuni, delivered thousands of babies and saved hundreds of women's lives. He was a counselor and father figure to many young men. He was a dedicated husband to Bogusia and father to Medzio and Marian. He was a kind grandfather to our boys. He was not the kind of man who I could say was "just a father-in-law" to me, since I could see the whole picture. He was all of these things (doctor, teacher, family patriarch, and trusted advisor) in an unparalleled, strong, and extraordinary way.

*Afterword*

# Living in America

I know, I should say "living in the United States of America." But the United States is referred to in Swahili as *Marekani*, America. I've lived in America for two years now. It doesn't feel strange anymore. I am not grieving for the scents and views I left behind, although I miss my friends. The vividness of the experience, the juxtaposition between Africa and America, has become muted. My kids no longer speak with a notably different accent, or unknowingly slip Swahili, Dutch, Afrikaans or British words into their conversation.

The strangeness and discomfort is gone. I live in a place where, by and large, people can pronounce my name. I no longer go by my Swahili-sized alias, Maria Pumpkin. I no longer have a voice in my head screaming "First world problem!" when someone insists on something that really seems like icing on the cake.

As life in the U.S. begins to come into focus, I start understanding that some of our "first world problems" can be huge. My friend's husband was detained to be deported to a country he hasn't visited in twenty-five years, leaving their three kids in a precarious financial situation. I volunteer at a prison and find out that a huge percentage of the men will be back in prison not long after they are released, when federal laws will keep them from voting, and prejudice will keep them from getting employment. My friend's son overdoses, and when I mention it in Quaker meeting, another grieving father breaks down and pulls out a picture of his eighteen-year-old son whom he also lost to heroin. And yet, here, we have many more resources to fight problems, and the freedom to discuss them, and many more options for solutions.

And through this, I think of my taxi driver telling me *safari ni hatua*, a journey is made up of steps. Take it slow, you will get there. You have to take many steps along the way. I am who I am due to the many steps I took in Africa, the daily stories that built my character, as well as the giant step I took to move back to the U.S.

# Acknowledgments

The short length of this book is disproportionate to the number of wonderful people who supported me through the years of living described. The most important acknowledgement of all is to my parents, Joel and Gretchen Plotkin. Thank you for fostering my love of writing and for orienting me, through your loving parenting, on a path which balanced reflection, caring, and action. As you celebrate your fiftieth wedding anniversary, I have never felt more certain that I have the best parents in the world.

There is nothing like being a mom to help me be present in the moment and conscious of my environment, both in Tanzania and the United States. Thank you to my boys, Janusz Fundikira Kumpuni and Tadzio Giryn Kumpuni, for giving me so much joy and letting me in on the secret of infinite love. *Nawapendeni milele wanangu.* I look forward to being part of your discoveries of your paths between and within your two countries, Tanzania and the United States.

I am also thankful to my former husband, Medzio Kumpuni. Our youth together and the years which followed were the reason I made Tanzania home. Although we are no longer married, we are forever friends and bonded by love for our boys. My life in Tanzania would not have happened without you.

Bogusia Kumpuni, my treasured mother-in-law, your adventurous story deserves an entire book of its own. Thank you for your love, your guidance in life in Tanzania, for inventing new recipes for your grandsons, and hundreds of Sunday dinners which made the whole week better.

My brother, Jeremy, and sister-in-law Audrey, have inspired me for years with their humor, caring, passion, and fun. Not only have they provided an example of a strong and happy marriage and excellent parenting, but also a way of living deliberately and well in the United States. I am so blessed to have been born with you waiting to be my older brother, Jeremy.

My West African years did not provide me with memories alone; they also gave me brothers. Haroun Hallack, whom I met in Sierra Leone in a village called Songo, emigrated to America shortly after I returned from West Africa. My family has been with him and his wife, Clarissa Matthews, through happy, fertile, heartbreaking, and triumphant times. Life cannot provide a richer gift than gaining a brother, and I am thankful for Haroun and Clarissa's place in our family. Losseni Koné, Celine Gougoua, and the entire Koné family from Ivory Coast have continually enriched my family's life with humor, adventure, kindness and lots of cashews.

While my year in West Africa was formative in my life, I recognize that my experience with the violent wars which erupted in Liberia and Sierra Leone was miniscule. Even that tiny glimpse was horrifying. I extend my deepest condolences to the people of Liberia and Sierra Leone who lived through or lost family and friends during those years, and thanks to the Roberts family of Monrovia who hosted me in 1989, and got me on that airplane out of Liberia in 1990.

Thanks to my Tanzanian friends, some of whom appear in this book and some who do not, but are nonetheless indelibly woven into the fabric of my life in Tanzania: Asma Ramadhan Khamis, Sarah George, Renatus Ideka and Angela Travis, Chris and Deryck Kilala, Caroline Batende, Yusuph Kulindwa, Victor Mponzi, Gregory Kabadi, Rita Mutayoba, John Charles, Giulia Besana, Dorica Boyee, Ruth Lemwayi, Flora Hezwa, Juliana Frederick, Zuwena Margreth, Angelister Mworia, Illuminata Sanga, Catherine Kahabuka, Albert Komba, Lemmy Mabuga, Fatma Kabole, Abdallah Jaffery, Charles Wanga, Masuma Mamdani, Ikupa Akim, Amuri Mbaraka, Ukende Shalla, Ansbert De Valk and Elsbeth Graswinkel, Peter Haule and Naoko Akiyama, and many more.

Dr. Bertha Maegga, the entomologist iron lady who supervised me conducting research in onchocerciasis in the mountains of Tukuyu in 1994; I am waiting for your book.

I am so grateful for my extended family in Africa, the other expatriates who were both teaching and learning with me. My sisters Ranahnah Ayodele Afriye, Anike Akridge, and Jackie Gayle Bony, you were as essential as the air I breathed and I could not have survived without you. Ranahnah, you truly **are** my sunshine. Jim Matuba and Cray Bony, I am so thankful to have two very kind and very tall little brothers (*leki ya ngai*). Isaka Kiroya, you are a great friend and an excellent example of how Masaai are the coolest. Judy Prince, you may move to Canada, but to me, you and your four boys will forever be from Iringa. Andrew Perkins and Nike Doggart, you were not just dedicated friends, you were my nature experts: you could answer any question, be it about primates or the forest. Rebecca Arnold, my gentle friend, I will forever remember driving you down the potholes of Migombani Street as fast as I could to get you to the hospital when you were in labor. Sara Collins, your grace, kindness and humor made you the Irish angel of Dar es Salaam, and not just my angel. Thank you to Maggie Bangser and Michelle Roland, who were there with me in the grieving process after losing

Gilly. Karren Kimesera, you are my sister born 12 days after me on another continent: My life would not be the same without you. Ndinini Kimesera, always the responsible older sister, the school you started for Masaai young women in Arusha is an inspiration. Natalie Hendler, Hally Mahler, Alysha Beyer, Jennifer Erie, Michael Lerner and Olga Torres, Anne and Rommert Schram, Suzan and Goodlove, Sundus and Robert, you all were indispensable to my life in Tanzania.

Dear friends helped me through the difficult transition of moving back to the United States: Bupe Mwambingu, you are the boys' favorite auntie with good reason. Your kindness shines so brightly. Chelu Mfalila, you are one of the smartest, sassiest women I know. To my amazing neighbor in Carrboro, Mariela Hernandez, who tackles life with a smile and ease, even in the face of incredible adversity: I have never met anyone as strong as you. Sean Chen, thank you for becoming my first new friend in Chapel Hill and for rescuing me with morning coffees. And topping it off by marrying the brilliant Lori Khamala. Thank you, John Doerfer, for your friendship. How could I have possibly asked for good whiskey, hilarious irreverence, keen insight, strong opinions, financial advice as well as dog-sitting, right across the street? I am so grateful to Kerry James and Mwenda Kudumu for the warmth, support, understanding and advice on how to be a great single mom. Great thanks to Karen Herring and Angela Wilson Crocker for demonstrating how to keep cool when parenting a teenager. Thanks to Aaron Huslage for your friendship and your amazing smarts. Peter and Tina Johnson, between delivering babies, improving educational design throughout the world, parenting a large and diverse group of kids, and occasionally wielding chainsaws, you have provided me with some of my life's best examples of how to be grown up and cool at the same time. Thanks to Jeff Ward and Sheena Currie for technical improvements in pharmacology and midwifery mentioned in this book. Thank you also to wonderful neighbors, Dena Bolton and Fernando Rubio, Lillian Mindich, Reade Oakley, Adrian and Silvana Moreno, Ana and Ted Calhoun, Alexandra Sheaves, Bonzi Crotty, Seval and Baris Deniz, Sara Skinner, Sarah and Charlie Hileman. Thanks to the entire Chapel Hill Friends Meeting, and especially Thomas McQuiston, Asta Crowe, Carolyn Stuart and Stacey Sewall.

*Oboto mingi* to my distinguished Lingala professor, Dr. Alphonse Mutima. When I miss Africa, I only have to go to your class.

To my Marlboro college friends, Rachel Aho, Corin Cummings, and Amy Daisy Heard, thanks for friendship which started out just seeming like fun and good times, but which have now provided me with over 20 years of backup and companionship. You also married smart and talented spouses: Eric Aho, Liesa Cummings, and Ando van der Velden.

And finally, last not being at all least, thank you to Milton D. Toro, who found me in a coffee shop and turned me into a princess.

## *About the Author*

Marya K. Plotkin grew up in a Quaker family amidst an overgrown Christmas tree farm in central New York State and left for West Africa after high school. She studied biology and international studies at Marlboro College in Vermont, then spent a year volunteering at a malaria research station in the Morogoro region of Tanzania.

After completing a master's degree in public health from the University of North Carolina-Chapel Hill in 1999, she was awarded a two-year international fellowship and moved to Tanzania to work with the African Medical Research Foundation (AMREF) conducting program monitoring and evaluation of a national HIV testing program.

She has worked with JSI, AMREF, and Concern Worldwide and currently works with Jhpiego, an affiliate of Johns Hopkins University, conducting research and program evaluation on programs to strengthen health systems in Africa.

In the course of more than eleven years in Tanzania, Marya worked on programs to prevent maternal and newborn mortality, HIV/AIDS, cervical cancer, and malaria in pregnancy. She has been first author or co-author on over a dozen articles in peer-reviewed scientific journals.

She lives in Chapel Hill, North Carolina, with her two sons, Janusz and Tadzio, and is currently studying in the Executive

Doctoral Program in Health Leadership program at UNC-Chapel Hill, learning the Lingala language, and conducting research and program evaluation for Jhpiego. She is fluent in Swahili.

Please visit Marya Plotkin's LinkedIn page for more details, linkedin.com/in-maryaplotkin.